AT MY TABLE

MARY McCARTNEY

Vegetarian Feasts for Family and Friends

Chatto & Windus
LONDON

1 3 5 7 9 10 8 6 4 2

Chatto & Windus, an imprint of Vintage,
20 Vauxhall Bridge Road,
London SW1V 2SA

Chatto & Windus is part of the Penguin Random House group of companies whose addresses can be found at global.penguinrandomhouse.com

 Penguin
Random House
UK

First published by Chatto & Windus in 2015

www.vintage-books.co.uk

A CIP catalogue record for this book is available from the British Library

ISBN 9780701189372

Art Direction and Design: ABOUD CREATIVE

Printed and bound by C&C Offset Printing Co., Ltd., China

Penguin Random House is committed to a sustainable future for our business, our readers and our planet. This book is made from Forest Stewardship Council® certified paper.

 FSC
www.fsc.org
MIX
Paper from
responsible sources
FSC® C008047

For my mum and dad, thank you for giving
me a passion for vegetarian cooking

CONTENTS

INTRODUCTION

Hello. I'm back with my second book and lots more ideas, ingredients and recipes that I'm really excited about. There are just so many great vegetarian options that I want to share with you.

When I was thinking about how to pull all these ideas together, I was struck by how important food is in terms of my own memories, of those magical moments that stand out over the years. Sharing a meal with family and friends is an opportunity to relax together, to laugh together and to bond together. Some of my happiest memories revolve around food, and I've tried to recreate those memories for my own children.

So what I decided to focus on for At My Table *was specific occasions. For me, food is such an important part of turning an event into something special. The love and passion that you put into cooking for people is repaid with great conversation and an empty plate – and lasting memories.*

So if my first book, Food, *was about individual dishes, this book is about showing that you can create a variety of complete vegetarian menus to complement a range of very different occasions – my way of showing how flexible vegetarian cooking can be! I love to plan menus, as it allows you to find the context for each individual dish, and the challenge was to create entire meals that would be delicious and satisfying for meat eaters and vegetarians alike. The menu plans are designed to inspire, and to help take away the stress of cooking for others.*

When we were growing up as a vegetarian family, we never felt we were missing out at mealtimes. But time and again, I come up against the idea that, without meat, a meal – and certainly a special or celebratory meal – is not complete. I hope that this book will show that there are endless and exciting possibilities for meat-free cooking, and enthuse many home cooks to try something new.

Of course I've added some photographs along the way to help tell the story.

Hope you enjoy

Love, Mary

COOKING NOTES

KEY SYMBOLS:

GF = gluten-free or can be adapted to be gluten-free
V+ = vegan or can be adapted to be vegan
DF = dairy-free or can be adapted to be dairy-free

Since I wrote my last book I have modified the way I eat. I've become a lot more interested in the science of food because I wanted to expand my knowledge of how to eat well and prepare tasty and satisfying meals while maximising the benefits to my health.

GLUTEN-FREE ALTERNATIVES

Gluten is the protein component found in grains such as wheat, rye and barley and it's also found in some oats. With the increased awareness of the health problems caused by coeliac disease and gluten sensitivity, there is now a good range of gluten-free alternatives available. I realised that I was eating a lot of gluten in my diet and it was starting to make me feel sluggish. After cutting back on gluten I felt more energetic and less bloated. So now, where I can, I always use gluten-free options and ingredients.

BUCKWHEAT FLOUR (gluten-free alternative to wheat or spelt flour): Despite the name, buckwheat is not a cereal grain, it is a fruit seed that is related to the rhubarb family and sorrel. I use buckwheat flour as a gluten-free alternative to wheat flour as it acts as a binding agent in sauces and in recipes such as my Courgette and Leek Fritters (p.178), Gluten-Free Seeded Bread (p.30) and in my cookies (see p.134, 139 and 199). I like to use Doves Farm buckwheat flour (they also make a wide range of other gluten-free flours).

MASA HARINA CORNFLOUR: Masa, the Spanish word for 'dough', is the traditional flour used to make corn tortillas. It is made with hominy, or dried corn kernels that have been soaked and cooked in lime water and then ground into masa.

MAIZE CORNMEAL FLOUR: Maize cornmeal flour is different from the purely starch, fine, white powder cornflour, which is separated from the protein and other components of maize flour. Maize cornmeal flour is the entire corn kernel milled into flour, and it contains protein. The grind can vary from fine to coarse (also known as polenta).

GLUTEN-FREE PASTRY: Gluten-free pastry mix is available; I use a brand called Helen's Pastry Mix to which you add butter, egg and water. This pastry will appear a little wet at first, but it will absorb the liquid while it is chilling in the fridge before you roll it out.

GLUTEN-FREE PASTA: You can now find a wide variety of gluten-free pastas, made from rice, corn, quinoa etc. My favourite variety is Doves Farm brown rice pasta.

TAMARI (alternative to soy sauce): Tamari is a liquid by-product of the fermentation process of miso. Tamari sauce is very similar in taste to soy sauce, and I like to use it to add flavour to recipes such as soups, gravy, roasts and stews. Tamari is usually gluten-free (but it's best to double-check the brand you purchase), unlike soy sauce, which contains wheat. Tamari has less salt and is a good source of B3, manganese and protein.

SUGAR CANE SWEETENER ALTERNATIVES

I have quite a sweet tooth, but try to moderate my sugar intake as it I know too much isn't healthy. One thing I try to do is use different types of sugars that either have an added health benefit or have a lower glycaemic index (a number associated with a food type that informs the food's effect on a person's blood sugar) than sugar cane, so I can avoid sugar spikes.

COCONUT SUGAR: I like to use coconut sugar as an alternative to cane sugar in recipes. It is made from the sap of the coconut palm, which is heated to evaporate the water and reduce it to granules. Coconut sugar is nutritious and has a lower glycaemic index than sugar cane, which means it does not cause such sugar spikes and crashes. It has a similar taste to brown sugar with a bit of a caramel flavour too.

MAPLE SYRUP: Maple syrup is a natural sweetener made from the sap of certain varieties of maple trees. Check the label to make sure you buy pure maple syrup and not maple-flavoured syrup. The latter is not pure as it is often made using flavoured refined sugar or high-fructose corn syrup. Pure maple syrup is pricey, but I think it's worth investing in as you can use it sparingly. It is very sweet and contains minerals such as manganese, magnesium, calcium and potassium. I love it best lightly drizzled over pancakes.

AGAVE: Agave syrup is the sweet syrup produced from several species of the agave plant. It has a lower glycaemic index than cane sugar and so causes less of a sugar spike. I like to use agave syrup instead of cane sugar to sweeten my luxury Hot Chocolate Milk (p.200) and Caramel Dipping Sauce (p.197). Agave is now available in many health-food shops and supermarkets.

HONEY: Honey has antioxidant and antibacterial properties. I keep a jar of runny honey in my store cupboard. Among many things, I like to use a little to stir into a tomato sauce to take away any acidity.

BLACKSTRAP MOLASSES: Molasses is a very dark, thick syrup which is a by-product of the sugar-refining process. It has a high mineral content and is a good source of iron. Molasses has a strong taste; to me it tastes a bit like liquorice.

HEALTHY FATS

The types of fats we eat really matter. For years I avoided all fats, thinking they would make me overweight and unhealthy. The more I looked into it I realised there are a variety of good fats that are really important to eat – monounsaturated fats, polyunsaturated fats and omega-3 fatty acids – as they help to protect our overall physical and emotional health. So now I make sure I include a good range of 'good' fats in my meals.

There are fats that are best avoided as they can have a negative effect on health. These are trans fats and saturated fats, which are reported to be unhealthy and can increase your 'bad' cholesterol levels.

GOOD MONOUNSATURATED FATS INCLUDE: avocados; olive oil; sunflower oil; sesame oil; olives; and nuts such as almonds, peanuts, macadamias, hazelnuts and cashews.

GOOD POLYUNSATURATED FATS INCLUDE: walnuts; pine nuts; and seeds such as sesame, sunflower, pumpkin and flax.

SOURCES OF OMEGA-3 FATTY ACIDS: flaxseed oil; hempseed oil; walnut oil; omega seed mix.

COOKING NOTES

DAIRY-FREE ALTERNATIVES

Since moderating the number of dairy products I eat I've discovered I have more energy. Also, growing numbers of people have found they are intolerant of or allergic to dairy. So I have worked a good variety of dairy-free alternatives into my everyday life. The good news is these are now more readily available than ever before.

ALMOND MILK: Almond milk is the dairy-free milk option I like to use most; it works well as a milk substitute in most aspects of cooking and I like its subtle flavour. I use it on breakfast cereals, in smoothies and when making my Quinoa Porridge (p.45). It is also a good source of vitamin E and is gluten-free.

RICE MILK: Rice milk is a thinner milk alternative. It doesn't have many extra minerals and vitamins so manufacturers often fortify it with extra calcium and vitamins. It is a good option if you have nut allergies and want gluten-free and low-fat alternatives.

SOYA CREAM: I use soya cream as a dairy cream alternative. When using it in cooking, I heat it gently before adding to hot ingredients, as I find that way it doesn't curdle. It works well in soups instead of dairy cream, and is good poured over desserts.

COCONUT OIL: Virgin coconut oil is now available in good health-food shops and is a good alternative to butter when baking.

DAIRY-FREE CHEESE: I don't use much dairy-free cheese, as I've not found many that I enjoy eating. However, my local health-food shop recently introduced me to the Violife range, which I do like, particularly their cheddar flavour slices, and these are also suitable for vegans.

PROTEINS

As a vegetarian, I pay attention to the proteins I eat, as plant-based proteins are not generally complete proteins (which means no one source provides all the amino acids you require). So, while there are many good vegetarian sources of protein, I try to eat different combinations of proteins from vegetables, grains, beans, legumes, nuts, seeds and eggs so I get a varied supply of protein sources in my diet. The added benefit is that most of these sources also provide a good amount of dietary fibre too.

QUINOA: Quinoa is a grain that is a complete protein as it contains all nine essential amino acids. It is also a good source of fibre and iron. I often cook up a batch of quinoa and keep it chilled in the fridge in an airtight container so I can add it to soups or salads as required. Also, I often use it instead of rice – it works well with my One-Pot Chilli (p.194) scooped on top to make a complete meal.

ORGANIC FREE-RANGE EGGS: For the recipes in this book that call for eggs I use organic free-range eggs, because they come from hens that are given organic feed and the hens are treated more humanely than caged hens as they are given outdoor space to roam around in. These eggs are a good source of amino acids, vitamins and minerals.

BLACK BEANS: These are a good source of protein, fibre and antioxidants.

CHICKPEAS: Chickpeas belong to the legume family and are good sources of protein, fibre, manganese and folate.

LENTILS: A great source of protein, lentils can also help to lower cholesterol because they contain plenty of soluble fibre.

FAVA BEANS: Also known as broad beans, fava beans contain protein and provide a good supply of vitamin K, vitamin B6, potassium, folate and fibre.

KIDNEY BEANS: These are a good source of protein, vitamin C, iron, folate and provide a good supply of dietary fibre.

CANNELLINI BEANS: Cannellini beans are a good source of protein, antioxidants and copper.

FROZEN PEAS: As well as being a good source of protein and antioxidants, these have anti-inflammatory properties and provide good amounts of vitamins B1, B2 , B3 and B6 and vitamin K.

BROWN RICE: Brown rice is a good source of selenium, manganese, antioxidants and dietary fibre.

FIRM TOFU: This is a good source of amino acids, iron and calcium.

ADDING FLAVOUR

NUTRITIONAL YEAST FLAKES: I sometimes use a spoonful of Engevita nutritional yeast flakes (by Marigold) to add flavour to a recipe such as veggie burgers or a roast. It is an inactive yeast that is rich in B vitamins. It has a cheese-like flavour, although it is dairy-free.

MARIGOLD REDUCED-SALT VEGETABLE BOUILLON: This is my preferred vegetable bouillon, which I often use as a vegetable stock for soups, gravies and in many other savoury recipes. I prefer this reduced-salt version, as I find many stock cubes and bouillons can be too salty.

CELEBRATION

BRUNCH

CELEBRATION BRUNCH

For 6

I absolutely love brunch: who wouldn't love a lazy late breakfast that you eat as the minutes tick towards lunchtime? At the weekend, I like to invite people over, buy the papers and make a selection of food for us all to choose from. But sometimes a special occasion calls for something extra, so this menu has a few twists and added ingredients to make it that little bit more celebratory.

MENU

Indulgent Chive Scrambled Eggs - GF, DF

Honey Lime Fruit Salad - GF, V+, DF

Medley of Muffins - DF

Pomegranate and Orange Prosecco Cocktail - GF, V+, DF

Gluten-Free Seeded Bread - GF, V+, DF

INDULGENT CHIVE SCRAMBLED EGGS

SERVES 1

Prep time: approx. 5 minutes
Cooking time: approx. 5 minutes
(slightly longer if you are cooking
for a large quantity of people)

INGREDIENTS

Per person:

2 large eggs

15g butter (or dairy-free alternative)

2 tablespoons milk or cream (or soya
   cream for a dairy-free option)

1 tablespoon finely chopped
   fresh chives

sea salt and freshly ground
   black pepper, to taste

GF, DF

How do you take an unbeatable classic like scrambled eggs and elevate it to something special? I have taken my inspiration from France. Using a whisk instead of a wooden spoon makes the eggs light and fluffy, and adding a herb, in this case chives, finishes the job beautifully. I love the added flavour and the pretty flecks of green.

METHOD

Crack the eggs into a mixing bowl, season with a little salt and pepper and beat with a hand whisk.

Melt the butter over a medium heat in a saucepan large enough to accommodate the number of eggs you are preparing, with enough room to be able to stir without spillage.

When the butter is melted, add the well-beaten eggs to the pan and stir with a hand whisk – this will ensure the eggs maintain a light texture.

As soon as the eggs begin to set, add the milk or cream and the chopped chives. Continue to stir with the whisk until the eggs reach a creamy consistency.

Serve immediately on hot buttered toast.

HONEY LIME FRUIT SALAD

SERVES 6

Prep time: 10 minutes

INGREDIENTS

300g pineapple, peeled and cored

1 medium ripe mango, peeled and
stone removed

2 kiwi fruit, peeled

180g strawberries (approx. 2 handfuls)

80g blueberries (approx. 2 handfuls),
stalks removed

For the dressing:

2 tablespoons freshly squeezed lime
juice (approx. 1 lime)

½–1 teaspoon finely grated fresh
ginger, to taste

1 tablespoon runny honey (or
agave syrup)

GF, V+, DF

For me, a brunch isn't complete without a great fruit salad. The colour and fragrance it brings to the table is amazing and it's something everyone will dip into. In this recipe, I've added a dressing of honey, ginger and fresh lime juice that brings extra punch to the salad.

METHOD

Chop the pineapple, mango and kiwi into small bite-sized cubes and put them into a medium serving bowl.

Hull and quarter the strawberries and add them to the bowl, along with the blueberries.

Combine all the dressing ingredients in a glass or small bowl, mixing well until the honey dissolves into the lime. Pour the dressing over the chopped fruit and stir gently to allow the flavours to infuse. Set to one side until ready to serve.

This salad is delicious served with plain yoghurt, chopped nuts and an extra drizzle of honey, or you can simply enjoy it on its own.

MEDLEY OF MUFFINS

MAKES 12
Prep time: 15 minutes
Cooking time: 20–25 minutes

INGREDIENTS

For the basic muffin mix:
2 large eggs
125ml vegetable oil
250ml milk (or almond milk for
  a dairy-free option)
200g caster sugar
400g plain, wholemeal or spelt flour
3 teaspoons baking powder
1 teaspoon salt

Pear & walnut muffin:
1 small pear, cored, peeled and
finely chopped, mixed with 50g
walnuts, finely chopped, and ½
teaspoon ground cinnamon

Berry muffin:
80g blueberries and/or raspberries

Lemon & poppy seed muffin:
zest of 1 lemon, juice of ½ lemon
and 1 teaspoon poppy seeds

DF

Freshly baked muffins are irresistible, but there are so many possible flavours – how do you choose? All my kids have a different favourite, of course. So, to get around the problem, I make a batch of the basic muffin mix, then divide the mixture into three separate bowls and add a different flavour to each bowl. These are our top three combinations, but you can play around and come up with your own.

METHOD

Preheat the oven to 200°C/gas mark 6. Line a 12-cup muffin tin with muffin cases.

In a mixing bowl or food processor, beat the eggs and then mix in the oil, milk and sugar. Sift in the dry ingredients and mix until well combined, but do not overbeat. Now that you have your basic muffin mix, you can get creative.

Divide the mixture equally between three bowls and add your preferred flavour ingredients. For instance, add the pear and walnuts to one, the mixed berries to another and, finally, the lemon zest and poppy seeds to the last one. Or come up with your own variations.

Spoon the mixture equally into the muffin cases – each bowl should have enough mixture for four muffins. As a rough guide, each muffin case should be around three-quarters full.

Bake in the middle of the oven for 20–25 minutes, or until a skewer comes out clean.

POMEGRANATE AND ORANGE PROSECCO COCKTAIL

SERVES 6

Prep time: 5 minutes

INGREDIENTS

750ml bottle Prosecco or Champagne
   or sparkling white wine
200ml pomegranate juice
100ml freshly squeezed orange juice

6 champagne flutes

GF, V+, DF

I was introduced to Prosecco at a friend's house a few years ago and find it a lighter and more drinkable sparkling wine than Champagne. It's also great mixed with fresh fruit juice and here I've chosen pomegranate and orange to give it a real zing for a brunch menu. (Of course you can use Champagne if you prefer.)

METHOD

Chill your Prosecco (or Champagne or sparkling wine) and the orange and pomegranate juices.

Pour the Prosecco into six champagne flutes first, filling each one about two-thirds full. Mix the orange and pomegranate juices together in a jug and use to top up each glass.

GLUTEN-FREE SEEDED BREAD

MAKES 1 LOAF
Prep time: 10 minutes
Resting time: 1½ hours
Cooking time: 30 minutes

INGREDIENTS
100g potato flour (starch)
100g buckwheat flour
100g cornmeal flour, plus
    more for dusting the tin
80g seeds (a mix of pumpkin seeds,
    sunflower seeds, pine nuts)
1½ teaspoons active dried yeast
400ml warm water
1 teaspoon salt
oil, for greasing the tin

GF, V+, DF

I love bread — in fact there are times when only bread will do. I love it toasted and I love it with eggs, I love it for sandwiches and I love it simply spread with hummous or butter. To cut down on my gluten intake, I have started making gluten-free bread at home. What I don't eat on the day of baking I slice, wrap in foil and keep in the freezer. Then it's there, ready sliced so I can put it straight in the toaster whenever I feel the need to indulge.

METHOD
Weigh out the flours and seeds into a medium mixing bowl and set aside. Put the active dried yeast into a medium-large mixing bowl and pour the warm water over it. Stir until the yeast has fully dissolved.

Using a wooden spoon, mix the flours, seeds and salt into the yeast water mixture. It should be the consistency of plain yoghurt; if not, you may need to add an extra tablespoon or so of water to achieve the right consistency. Cover the bowl with a clean tea towel and leave to rest in a warm place for 1 hour.

In the meantime, grease a 20 x 10cm loaf tin and dust with corn meal flour (this is to avoid the bread sticking to the tin when turning it out after baking). Then pour the mixture into the prepared loaf tin, cover again with the tea towel and allow it to rest for a further 30 minutes.

Preheat the oven to 240°C/gas mark 9. Pour a couple of cups of water into a roasting tray and place the loaf tin in the tray. Put the tray in the oven, and turn the temperature down to 220°C/gas mark 7. Bake for 30 minutes, until golden and a skewer comes out clean.

Turn the loaf out of the tin onto a wooden board and allow to cool. You will need to use a sharp bread knife to slice it, as the crust is quite crisp.

ENERGY
BREAKFAST

ENERGY BREAKFAST

For 2–4

For me, breakfast is the most important meal of the day. If I eat well in the morning, I'm set up for the day and much less likely to eat badly. So, here, I've created a menu that delivers on flavour and gives a powerful energy boost to kick off the day. You can choose one recipe from the menu each day, to keep your week varied, or make them all at once! Your choice.

MENU

Buckwheat Pancakes - GF, DF

Sliced Avocado and Soft-Boiled Eggs on Toast - GF, DF

Quinoa Porridge - GF, V+, DF

Energy Breakfast Smoothie - GF, V+, DF

BUCKWHEAT PANCAKES

MAKES 14–16 PANCAKES
approx. 9cm in diameter (you can
freeze any leftovers)
Prep time: 10 minutes
Cooking time: 10 minutes

INGREDIENTS
120g buckwheat flour
½ teaspoon bicarbonate of soda
3 teaspoons baking powder
2 large eggs, separated
200ml milk (or almond or soya milk
    for dairy-free option)
1 tablespoon melted butter or
    coconut oil
10g butter, or 2 teaspoons coconut
    oil, for frying
maple syrup, for drizzling on top

GF, DF

Buckwheat flour contains no gluten, although the name implies otherwise. Folding in the whisked egg whites ensures these pancakes retain a light taste and the maple syrup makes them irresistible. I usually serve four pancakes per person. If you are gluten intolerant, double check that your baking powder is gluten-free.

METHOD
Preheat the oven to 160°C/gas mark 3. Prepare a baking tray with foil to wrap the pancakes in, to keep them warm while you cook the rest of the batch.

Sift the buckwheat flour, bicarbonate of soda and baking powder together into a medium mixing bowl and make a well in the centre of the flour. Using a wooden spoon or hand whisk, mix the egg yolks and milk together in a medium bowl, and then gradually pour into the well of flour, beating all the time to avoid lumps. Stir in the tablespoon of melted butter or oil and continue to beat until your batter is a smooth, creamy consistency.

In a separate, medium mixing bowl, use a hand whisk or electric mixer to whisk the egg whites until they form soft peaks. Gently fold these whites into the batter, using a metal spoon and being careful not to beat all the air out of the mix – this will ensure light, fluffy pancakes.

Preheat a large, non-stick frying pan over a medium heat. Add a little butter or coconut oil to form a light glaze over the base of the pan. You can tell if it is hot enough to start cooking your pancakes by dropping a tiny amount of batter into the pan – if it sizzles, you are ready to go.

Pour the batter into the pan – 2 tablespoons per pancake, or if you have one to hand, a quarter-cup measure is ideal. Depending on the size of your pan, you can probably cook in batches of three or four. But don't overcrowd your pan, as it will make it more difficult to flip the pancakes over. When small bubbles start to appear on the surface of the pancakes, gently lift the edges with a spatula and check that the underside is golden brown. Then flip them over and cook until the other side is golden too and the pancakes are cooked through. Whenever the pan goes dry, add a little extra oil or butter and re-glaze the base before continuing. As you go, transfer the cooked pancakes to the baking tray, cover with foil and place in the oven to keep warm until all the batter has been used up.

Serve the pancakes drizzled with maple syrup and maybe some fresh berries or chopped banana. If you have some pancakes left over, you can wrap them in foil and freeze them – reheat from frozen, in a warm oven, as required.

SLICED AVOCADO AND SOFT-BOILED EGGS ON TOAST

SERVES 2

Prep time: 10 minutes
Cooking time: 10 minutes

INGREDIENTS

2 large eggs
1 ripe avocado
juice of ½ lemon or 1 lime
¼ teaspoon red chilli flakes or ½
 teaspoon chopped and deseeded
 fresh red chilli or, if preferred,
 ½ teaspoon chopped fresh chives
2 slices of bread, such as multigrain,
 wholemeal or gluten-free
 (see recipe, p.30)
butter or spread, for the toast
sea salt and freshly ground black
 pepper, to taste

GF, DF

I started to see avocado and egg on toast crop up quite often on restaurant and café menus. I didn't think I would like the combination, but when I tried it I loved it!

METHOD

For the soft-boiled eggs, fill a small saucepan with water and bring to the boil. Using a spoon, gently slide in the eggs and boil for 6 minutes. Turn off the heat, lift the eggs out with the spoon and plunge into cold water for a couple of seconds to stop further cooking and allow the eggs to cool enough so that you can peel off the shell.

Meanwhile, halve the avocado, remove the stone and carefully scoop out the flesh. Slice each half thinly, and place on a plate. Lightly squeeze with lemon or lime juice and sprinkle with the chilli or chives.

Now toast your bread and lightly butter it. Gently arrange half an avocado on top of each piece of toast. Peel the warm boiled eggs and lay one on top of each piece of avocado toast, breaking the egg in half with a knife to allow the yolk to spill out. Add a grind of black pepper and a sprinkle of sea salt. Ready to eat.

QUINOA PORRIDGE

SERVES 2

Prep time: 5 minutes

Cooking time: 20 minutes

INGREDIENTS

90g uncooked white quinoa, rinsed

300ml milk (or unsweetened almond milk for dairy-free option; if using sweetened almond milk, there's no need for the 1 tablespoon of maple syrup/honey)

100ml water

1 tablespoon maple syrup or runny honey, plus more for drizzling on top

½ teaspoon cinnamon

1 teaspoon vanilla extract

Ideas for toppings:

handful of fresh berries (raspberries, blueberries, strawberries)

chopped pear

chopped banana

chopped walnuts

hulled hemp seeds

GF, V+, DF

Porridge made with quinoa is a great alternative to traditional oats. There are many reasons why I like to use quinoa. It's a gluten-free grain, it's a complete protein, containing all nine essential amino acids, and it's a good source of iron, fibre and magnesium. Used in this recipe, it also makes for a satisfying, energy-boosting breakfast.

METHOD

In a medium saucepan mix together the uncooked quinoa, milk, water, maple syrup, cinnamon and vanilla extract.

Bring to the boil, then turn down the heat to low. Cover and simmer gently for about 20 minutes, stirring occasionally, until the quinoa has absorbed the milk and has the consistency of porridge. (If you prefer a thicker consistency, you can remove the lid and simmer for a few extra minutes.)

Divide between two bowls and drizzle with a little extra maple syrup or runny honey. Sprinkle with your desired toppings.

ENERGY BREAKFAST SMOOTHIE

SERVES 1

Prep time: 5 minutes

INGREDIENTS

200ml almond milk, rice milk or
  dairy milk

½ tablespoon pumpkin seeds

1 tablespoon hemp seeds

1 tablespoon pine nuts

1 ripe banana

1 kiwi, peeled (optional)

1 scoop whey or protein powder, such
  as Spiru-Tein (optional; available in
  health-food shops or online)

GF, V+, DF

The mornings can be such a rush, so I find the best way to take on board many of the nutrients I need to get through the day is to have a quick smoothie for breakfast. You can jam in all the healthy stuff and make it super-tasty too. In this recipe I use pine nuts, because they have so many health benefits, being rich in essential minerals and vitamins and mono-unsaturated fatty acids. (I keep a little pack of pine nuts in my handbag to snack on throughout the day, too.) I also add protein to my smoothie to make it a complete breakfast. There are many powdered proteins available, from whey to hemp, but I usually use a non-dairy option called Spiru-Tein.

METHOD

For the quick version, put all the ingredients into a blender and whizz until smooth – about 20–30 seconds.

However, if you have time the night before, pop the seeds and pine nuts into your milk and leave in the fridge overnight. Peel and chop the banana and keep it in the freezer overnight. Soaking the seeds and nuts will cause them to swell and soften, making them easier to digest. Frozen banana creates a much creamier, colder smoothie.

At breakfast time, add the chopped kiwi – and the protein, if using – to all the prepared ingredients in the blender and go!

MIDDLE EASTERN

FEAST

MIDDLE EASTERN FEAST

For 4–6

There are two reasons why I have a real passion for Middle Eastern food. Firstly, there are just so many great vegetarian options that I keep going back to again and again. Secondly, my father-in-law (who, unfortunately, I never met) was Lebanese, so this menu plan is dedicated to his memory.

MENU

Hummous - GF, V+, DF

Baba Ganoush - GF, V+, DF

Tabouleh - GF, V+, DF

Falafels - GF, V+, DF

Lentils and Rice with Caramelised Onions - GF, V+, DF

Loubieh Bel Zeit (green beans in tomato sauce) - GF, V+, DF

Moussaka - GF

Nutty Baklava

HUMMOUS

SERVES 4–6
Prep time: 5 minutes

INGREDIENTS
400g tin chickpeas
4 tablespoons sunflower or
    extra-virgin olive oil
3 tablespoons tahini paste
4 tablespoons freshly squeezed
    lemon juice (approx. 2 lemons)
2 small cloves garlic, peeled
½ teaspoon sea salt
2 tablespoons water

To garnish (optional):
extra-virgin olive oil
lightly toasted pine nuts
paprika
chopped fresh parsley

GF, V+, DF

Hummous is a staple in my family and we all love it – in sandwiches, on toast, scooped up with crisps or vegetable sticks. Whichever way you choose to serve it, it tastes so good! It's easy to make, healthy and you can always add your own twist to this recipe by blending in a spoonful of pumpkin seeds, sundried tomato, avocado, or whatever takes your fancy. It's packed with nutrients too, being a good source of protein, fibre and healthy essential fats.

METHOD
Drain the chickpeas and rinse them briefly under cold running water. Tip the chickpeas into a food processor. Add the oil, tahini paste, lemon juice, garlic, sea salt and water.

Blitz for about 1 minute until smooth and creamy.

For a delicious finishing touch, if you like, drizzle with extra-virgin olive oil and top with a scattering of toasted pine nuts, a light dusting of paprika or some freshly chopped parsley.

BABA GANOUSH

SERVES 4
Prep time: 10 minutes
Cooking time: 40–45 minutes

INGREDIENTS

2 large aubergines (approx. 600g)
2 cloves garlic, finely chopped
pinch sea salt, or to taste
¼ teaspoon smoked paprika
2 tablespoons freshly squeezed
   lemon juice (approx. 1 lemon)
2 tablespoons tahini paste, or more
   to taste

To garnish (optional):
extra-virgin olive oil
fresh pomegranate seeds
chopped mint leaves

GF, V+, DF

This smoky-flavoured dip comprises roasted aubergines mixed with tahini, lemon juice and garlic. I love it served alongside bowls of vegetable sticks and toasted pittas or flatbread, ready for scooping it up.

METHOD

Preheat the grill to medium-high. Place the aubergines directly on a baking tray and grill them, turning every 5 minutes until the skins are charred and black all over. (Alternatively, if you have a gas hob or are having a summer barbecue, hold the aubergines with metal tongs over the open flame, turning them regularly, for about 5 minutes, until the skin is charred and blistered. This will give an extra smoky flavour to the finished dish. Then place on a baking tray.)

Preheat the oven to 200°C/gas mark 6. Place the baking tray in the centre of the oven and bake the aubergines for 40 minutes, until they are soft and cooked through.

Remove from the oven and allow to cool. Then cut open the aubergines and scoop out the insides into a colander or sieve, allowing any extra juices to drain away. Put the aubergine filling into a food processor or medium bowl.

Add the chopped garlic, sea salt, smoked paprika, lemon juice and tahini paste and blitz in the food processor for about 5 seconds. Or mash by hand with a fork until you achieve a smooth consistency.

Serve just as it is, or with a drizzle of extra-virgin olive oil, some fresh pomegranate seeds and a few shredded fresh mint leaves sprinkled on top.

TABOULEH

SERVES 4

Prep time: 15 minutes
Standing time: 10 minutes
Cooking time: 15 minutes

INGREDIENTS

100g uncooked white quinoa (for
    gluten-free option), rinsed, or
    bulgur wheat
200ml water
3 medium ripe red tomatoes,
    deseeded and diced
3 spring onions, finely chopped
150g cucumber (approx. ½), diced
100g fresh flat-leaf parsley,
    finely chopped
3 tablespoons finely chopped fresh
    mint (small handful)
sea salt and freshly ground black
    pepper, to taste

For the dressing:

4 tablespoons extra-virgin olive oil
3 tablespoons freshly squeezed
    lemon juice (approx. 1½ lemons)
pinch sea salt

GF, V+, DF

This refreshing salad combines lots of chopped fresh parsley and vibrant, ripe tomatoes with a tangy citrus lemon dressing. Traditionally it's made with bulgur wheat but I like to use cooked quinoa instead, as I think it works well and has the added advantage of being a gluten-free superfood.

METHOD

Place the quinoa (or bulgur wheat) in a medium saucepan, then cover with the water. Bring to the boil, cook for 15 minutes, then take off the heat and cover with a tea towel to absorb the steam. Allow to stand for 10 minutes. Remove the tea towel and fork through – the quinoa should be light with the grains separated. Allow to cool.

Meanwhile, put the tomatoes, spring onions and cucumber into a large mixing bowl.

Mix the dressing ingredients in a cup or small bowl and whisk with a fork for a few seconds until smooth.

When ready to serve, tip the cooled quinoa and the chopped herbs into the large bowl with the tomatoes, spring onions and cucumber. Pour over the dressing, season with salt and pepper and toss well.

FALAFELS

MAKES APPROX. 10 FALAFELS

Prep time: 15 minutes

Chilling time: 1 hour

Cooking time: 10 minutes

INGREDIENTS

1 tablespoon vegetable oil

1 small onion, finely chopped

1 clove garlic, finely chopped

150g tinned chickpeas, drained
   and rinsed

150g fresh or frozen broad beans,
   defrosted if frozen

1 spring onion, finely chopped

2 tablespoons finely chopped fresh
   parsley or coriander

1 teaspoon ground cumin

1 teaspoon ground tumeric

1 teaspoon sea salt

½ teaspoon cayenne pepper

flour (plain or buckwheat), for dusting

vegetable oil for frying

GF, V+, DF

These falafels are made using a mixture of blended chickpeas and broad beans, flavoured with delicate spices and herbs. They are packed with protein and so versatile – try them with dips such as hummous, or stuffed into pitta bread with some crisp salad leaves tossed in a lemon tahini dressing. The list goes on... I always make extra to snack on throughout the week.

METHOD

Heat 1 tablespoon of vegetable oil in a large pan and fry the onion and garlic over a medium heat for 3-4 minutes, or until softened, then remove from the heat.

Tip the onion and garlic into a food processor and add the chickpeas, beans, spring onion, herbs, spices and seasoning. Pulse until well combined and chopped fine. (If you don't have a food processor, just chop everything together very small.) Take 1 heaped tablespoon of the falafel mixture at a time and, using your hands (rinsed in cold water), shape into balls, flattening each one slightly to make a patty shape. You should be able to make about 10 balls out of this amount. Leave to chill in the fridge for 1 hour.

When ready to cook, transfer the falafels to a chopping board and lightly dust all over with flour.

Pour enough vegetable oil into a deep frying pan so the oil is about 3mm deep, and heat until it is hot. To test if it's hot enough, add a small drop of the mixture to the pan and if it sizzles, the oil is ready.

Fry the falafels (you may need to do this in batches) for about 1 minute on each side, until golden. Remove and drain on kitchen paper and repeat until all the falafels are cooked.

Good served with Hummous (p.54) or salad.

LENTILS AND RICE
WITH CARAMELISED ONIONS

SERVES 4
Prep time: 15 minutes
Cooking time: 30–45 minutes,
    depending on rice cooking time

INGREDIENTS
100g brown rice
250ml hot vegetable stock
200g dried green lentils, rinsed
2 tablespoons light olive oil or
    vegetable oil
3 medium onions (you could use 2
    red onions and one white onion),
    halved and thinly sliced
1 teaspoon ground cumin
¼ teaspoon ground cinnamon
2 tablespoons chopped fresh parsley
pinch sea salt and freshly ground
    black pepper, to taste
squeeze of fresh lemon juice

GF, V+, DF

This lentil and rice mixture is mildly flavoured with cumin and topped with sweet, caramelised onions. Its delicate flavour forms the perfect complement to the juicy tomato sauce in the Loubieh Bel Zeit (p.64).

METHOD
Place the rice in a medium saucepan and pour in the hot vegetable stock. Bring to the boil and then turn down to a gentle bubbling simmer. Cover with a lid and cook for 25–40 minutes according to the packet instructions. All of the liquid will be absorbed and the rice should be just tender (add more stock as required until the rice is cooked through). Then remove the lid, turn off the heat and cover with a tea towel to absorb the steam.

While the rice is cooking, put the lentils into a medium saucepan and pour in enough water to cover them by 3cm. Bring to the boil, then turn the heat down to a gentle simmer and allow the lentils to cook for about 15–20 minutes, until just cooked through. Drain in a sieve and set aside.

Meanwhile, heat the oil in a medium-large frying pan. Add the sliced onions, cumin and cinnamon. Cook over a medium heat, stirring often, for about 15–20 minutes, until the onions are caramelised and slightly crispy and darker in colour.

When the rice is ready, gently stir in the lentils, chopped parsley and two-thirds of the cooked onions, reserving the rest for the garnish. Stir gently and season with a little sea salt and freshly ground black pepper to taste. Top with the remaining onions and a squeeze of lemon juice, and serve.

LOUBIEH BEL ZEIT
(GREEN BEANS IN TOMATO SAUCE)

SERVES 4
Prep time: 10 minutes
Cooking time: 30 minutes

INGREDIENTS

500g ripe tomatoes, skinned and
    chopped (see right), or 400g
    tinned chopped tomatoes
2 tablespoons olive oil
500g green beans, topped and tailed
2 medium onions, finely chopped
4 cloves garlic, finely chopped
1 tablespoon tomato purée
½ tablespoon grated fresh ginger
¼ teaspoon ground cinnamon
¼ teaspoon ground coriander
200ml water
sea salt and freshly ground black
    pepper, to taste

GF, V+, DF

An all-time favourite! Fresh green beans cooked in a deliciously simple tomato sauce. This dish makes a great accompaniment to the Lentils and Rice with Caramelised Onions (p.63).

METHOD

To skin fresh tomatoes, prick them with a fork and plunge them into a pan of boiling water for about 5 minutes, or until the skin starts to split. Remove the tomatoes with a spoon and allow to cool, before peeling away the outer skin and chopping finely.

Heat 1 tablespoon of the olive oil in a medium-large frying pan and fry the green beans gently for about 2 minutes on a low-medium heat. Transfer the beans to a plate and set aside.

Meanwhile heat the remaining tablespoon of oil in the frying pan. Add the chopped tomatoes and onions, sauté gently for 5 minutes, then add the garlic, tomato purée, ginger, ground cinnamon and coriander and mix together well. Simmer gently for 10 minutes over a low heat, stirring often.

Add the green beans to the tomato mixture along with the 200ml of water. Cover and simmer gently for a further 15 minutes. Season with a pinch of sea salt and freshly ground black pepper to taste. This can be eaten warm, or more traditionally, at room temperature.

MOUSSAKA

SERVES 6

Prep time: 45 minutes
Cooking time: 30–40 minutes

INGREDIENTS

4 tablespoons olive oil

2 medium onions, halved and
thinly sliced

100g mushrooms, thinly sliced

2 cloves garlic, finely chopped

1 tablespoon tamari (for gluten-free
option) or soy sauce

200ml red wine

400g tin chopped tomatoes

200g tinned chickpeas, drained
and rinsed

200g tinned green lentils, drained
and rinsed

2 bay leaves

2 large potatoes (approx. 500g)

2 large aubergines (approx. 600g)

2 tablespoons chopped fresh herbs,
such as parsley and thyme, or 2
teaspoons dried mixed herbs

sea salt and freshly ground black
pepper, to taste

For the sauce:

50g butter or vegetable oil

50g buckwheat flour (for gluten-free
option) or plain or spelt flour

600ml milk

150g mature Cheddar, grated

100g feta cheese

¼ teaspoon nutmeg

freshly ground black pepper

2 large eggs, beaten

GF

This vegetarian version of the classic recipe gets great feedback from both veggies and meat eaters alike. It is hearty, warming and satisfying.

METHOD

Preheat the oven to 180°C/gas mark 4 and lightly oil a 30 x 20cm oven dish or non-stick roasting tray.

In a medium saucepan, heat 2 tablespoons of the olive oil, then add the sliced onions and sauté for a couple of minutes. Add the mushrooms, garlic and tamari (or soy sauce) and allow to cook gently for 10 minutes, stirring often.

Stir in the wine and simmer for 1 minute to allow the alcohol to cook off. Add the tomatoes, chickpeas, lentils and bay leaves, stir well and season with salt and pepper. Simmer for 20 minutes, adding a little water – around 2 tablespoons at a time – if the sauce gets too thick.

Meanwhile, cut the potatoes into rounds about 1cm thick. Put into a medium pan of cold water, bring to the boil and parboil them for 10 minutes, then drain.

Prepare the aubergines by trimming off the woody ends and then slicing into approximately 1cm-thick rounds. Lay the potatoes and sliced aubergines on two greased non-stick baking trays, brush them with the remaining oil and sprinkle with the herbs. Bake for about 30 minutes, turning them once halfway through cooking, until golden.

Now turn to your white sauce. Melt the butter (or oil) in a medium saucepan over a low heat. Add the flour, stirring with a wooden spoon to form a paste. Take the pan off the heat and gradually add the milk a little at a time, stirring with a hand whisk to keep the sauce smooth and lump-free. Put the pan back over a medium heat, bring to a gentle simmer and cook for 2–4 minutes, stirring continuously, until the sauce has thickened. Add two-thirds of the grated Cheddar and crumble in the feta cheese, then stir until the cheese has melted. Add the nutmeg and freshly ground black pepper to taste and allow to cool slightly before finally beating in the eggs.

To assemble: pour half the tomato sauce into the prepared oven dish, followed by a generous layer of roasted potatoes and aubergines (about half the vegetables). Repeat with another layer of tomato sauce and the rest of the vegetable slices. Top with the white sauce and sprinkle with the remaining grated cheese. Bake for 30-40 minutes until golden and bubbly.

NUTTY BAKLAVA

MAKES 48 PIECES

Prep time: 30 minutes
Cooking time: 35–40 minutes
Cooling and setting time: 4–6 hours

INGREDIENTS

300g chopped mixed nuts (almonds,
    walnuts, pistachios or a combination
    of your favourite nuts)
50g dark brown sugar
½ teaspoon ground cinnamon
¼ teaspoon ground cloves
¼ teaspoon ground cardamom
150g butter
250g shop-bought filo pastry sheets
1–2 tablespoons finely chopped
    pistachios, for sprinkling on top

For the syrup:

1 cinnamon stick
100g dark brown sugar
1 tablespoon fresh lemon juice
    (approx. ½ lemon)
5 tablespoons honey
120ml water

I can't resist these bite-sized, indulgent, sweet pastries. They're made using layers of filo pastry, chopped nuts and a gorgeous sticky, sweet syrup poured over them. The perfect end to a wonderful Middle Eastern Feast.

METHOD

Preheat the oven to 180°C/gas mark 4 and lightly grease a baking tray (about 30 x 20cm). Chop the nuts into small pieces, either using a large knife or by pulsing in a food processor, being very careful not to grind them to dust. Put the nuts in a medium mixing bowl. Mix in the sugar, cinnamon, ground cloves and cardamom. Melt the butter in a small pan over a low heat.

Unwrap your filo sheets and cut them to fit the baking tray - most commercial brands are 60 x 40cm and contain between 8 and 10 sheets per 250g pack, so you can simply cut them in half. Cover your pastry sheets with a lightly dampened, clean tea towel to prevent the pastry from drying out while you work. Place one sheet of filo pastry on the baking tray and, using a pastry brush, brush with melted butter. Repeat until your pile of pastry is eight sheets thick, each sheet brushed with butter. Spoon on half of the nut mixture and spread evenly over the prepared filo pastry. Cover with two more sheets of filo, brushing each one with butter.

Now spoon the other half of the nut mixture on top and then top with another eight filo sheets, again ensuring that each sheet is brushed with the melted butter. Cut into 2.5cm squares, using a sharp knife - this size baking tray should hold approximately 48. Bake for 35–40 minutes until lightly golden brown and slightly crisp.

While your baklava is cooking, make the syrup. Put all the syrup ingredients into a small saucepan. Bring to the boil, then reduce to medium-low heat and simmer for about 7 minutes, until slightly thickened and reduced. Remove the cinnamon stick and allow to cool.

Once the baklava is cooked, take it out of the oven and, while it is still hot, spoon the cooled syrup along the cut lines between the squares. Use every last drop. Sprinkle the chopped pistachios over the top while it is still sticky with syrup. Leave for 4–6 hours to cool and set. You'll be amazed how quickly 48 squares of this yummy treat will disappear.

MY AMERICAN SIDE

(BBQ) FEAST

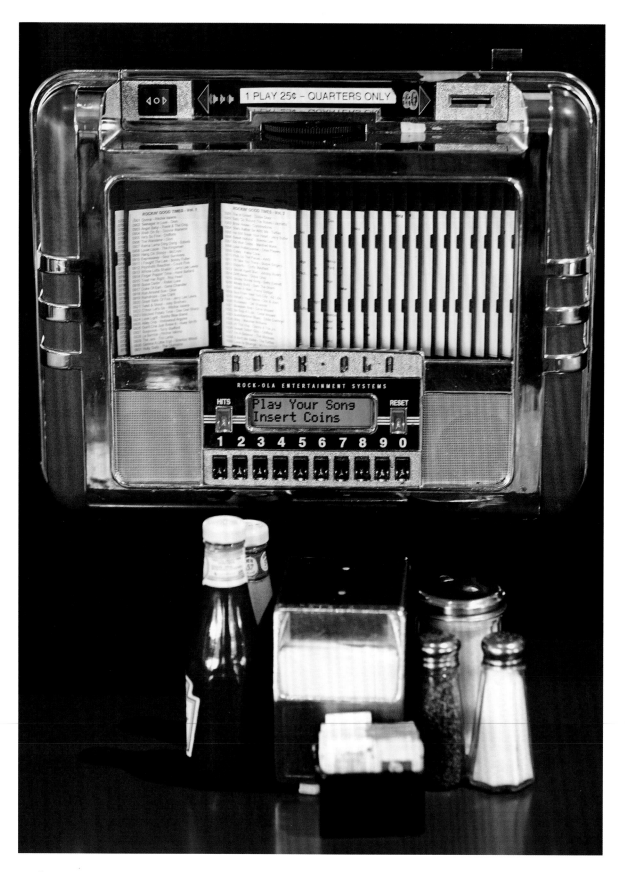

MY AMERICAN SIDE

As my dad's from Liverpool and my mum was from America, I grew up telling anyone who asked where I was from that I was half American and half Liverpudlian. Mum was the main cook in our home, and my cooking style is influenced and inspired by her. This menu is based around what we would make for a barbecue at home. As a vegetarian family, we never liked to feel we were missing out by not eating meat. Traditionally, Dad is in charge of the barbecue when we make this wonderful feast.

MENU

Black Bean Burgers - GF, V+, DF

Thousand Island Dressing - GF, V+, DF

Eggless Mayonnaise - GF, V+, DF

Creamy Dill Potato Salad - GF, V+, DF

Chuck It In Chef's Salad - GF, V+, DF

Sweet Potato Oven Chips - GF, V+, DF

Sweetcorn with Savoury Parsley Butter - GF, V+, DF

Key Lime and Coconut Pie - GF

BLACK BEAN BURGERS

MAKES 6 BURGERS
approx. 8cm wide and 1.5cm thick

Prep time: 20–30 minutes

Chilling time: 1 hour minimum

Cooking time: 5–10 minutes

INGREDIENTS

400g tin black beans or kidney
   beans, drained

2 tablespoons light olive oil,
   or 30g butter

1 medium red onion, finely chopped

140g mushrooms, finely chopped

2 tablespoons tamari (for gluten-free
   option) or soy sauce

1 clove garlic, finely chopped

1 tablespoon chopped fresh parsley,
   or 1 teaspoon dried mixed herbs

1 spring onion, finely chopped

½ teaspoon chilli flakes (optional)

4 tablespoons buckwheat flour
   (for gluten-free option) or plain or
   spelt flour

1 tablespoon nutritional yeast flakes,
   or ½ teaspoon Marmite (optional)

freshly ground black pepper, to taste

3 tablespoons vegetable oil (if not
   cooking on the barbecue), for frying

GF, V+, DF

I make these burgers with black beans because they are packed with protein and fibre. If you don't have black beans, then kidney beans are a great alternative. I love them sandwiched between a burger bun with all the toppings – sliced pickles, tomato, onion, lettuce, melted cheese, Thousand Island dressing (or mayo and ketchup) and mustard. My advice is to never skimp on the toppings!

METHOD

Put the beans into a large bowl and roughly mash them with a potato masher, or blend them in a food processor for a few seconds. You want them to keep some texture, so do not over-mash.

Heat the olive oil (or butter) in a medium frying pan, then sauté the onion for 3 minutes. Add the mushrooms and tamari (or soy sauce) and fry for a few more minutes, until most of the mushroom juice has evaporated.

Stir in the garlic, herbs, spring onion, chilli flakes and mashed beans, then allow the mixture to cook for about 2 minutes, stirring often. Transfer the mixture to a bowl and leave to cool slightly before mixing in the flour, nutritional yeast flakes (or Marmite) and black pepper to taste.

Divide the mixture into six portions and, using your hands, mould each portion into a patty shape (about 1.5cm thick and 8cm wide). Leave to chill in the fridge for at least 1 hour. To fry the burgers, heat the 3 tablespoons of vegetable oil in a medium-large frying pan and cook the burgers over a medium heat for about 2 minutes on each side, or until cooked through.

If cooking on the barbecue, chill the burgers in the fridge or freeze them for a couple of hours so they become firm. Then grill on both sides until golden brown and cooked through.

THOUSAND ISLAND DRESSING

SERVES 4
Prep time: 5 minutes

INGREDIENTS

4 tablespoons mayonnaise
1½ teaspoons tomato ketchup
1½ teaspoons tomato purée
1½ teaspoons capers or pickled
  gherkins, finely chopped
squeeze of fresh lemon juice
  (approx. 1 teaspoon)
small pinch sea salt and freshly
  ground black pepper, if desired

GF, V+, DF

This tangy dressing is great drizzled on top of the Black Bean Burgers (p.76). But it's so versatile, I love to use it on salads and in sandwiches, too – it can help turn a simple cheese sandwich into a work of art! (Use the Eggless Mayonnaise below for a dairy-free dressing.)

METHOD

Mix all the ingredients together in a small serving bowl. This dressing is delicious spooned over veggie burgers or served as a dip with crudités. I also love it drizzled on the leftover festive roast the next day. Any leftover dressing can be stored in an airtight container in the fridge for up to 4 days.

EGGLESS MAYONNAISE

MAKES APPROX. 150ML
Prep time: 5 minutes

INGREDIENTS

120ml sunflower oil
1 teaspoon Dijon or English mustard
1 tablespoon apple cider or white
  wine vinegar
2 tablespoons water
½ teaspoon sea salt
½ tablespoon ground/milled
  flaxseed (bought pre-ground)

GF, V+, DF

Let's face it, you can buy good-quality mayonnaise in most shops now. But sometimes it just feels more special to make your own. This mayo recipe leaves out the eggs and, instead, uses ground flaxseed, which I have in my store cupboard to add to smoothies for extra fibre and omega 3 benefits. I use this for dressings and in sandwiches, or just dolloped on the side of a baked potato with a big chopped salad.

METHOD

This technique uses an immersion stick blender. Pour the sunflower oil into a tall plastic jug or similar container, then add the mustard, vinegar, water, salt and ground flaxseed. Take the stick blender and put it into the jug so that it sits firmly on the bottom. Start to whisk on a high speed (there is probably only one speed). This will create a vortex that will draw the oil down. It should thicken up within a few seconds, and once it has thickened you can move the hand whisk around to ensure all the oil is blended. Serve or store in a sealed jar in the fridge, where it will keep for up to 1 week.

CREAMY DILL POTATO SALAD

SERVES 4–6
Prep time: 15 minutes
Cooking time: 15–20 minutes

INGREDIENTS
600g new potatoes
1 stick celery, finely chopped

For the dressing:
2 tablespoons mayonnaise or
   crème fraîche
2 tablespoons finely chopped fresh dill
1 spring onion, finely chopped, or
   1 tablespoon finely chopped
   red onion
1 teaspoon Dijon wholegrain mustard
1 tablespoon chopped
   gherkins/cornichons
½ teaspoon freshly squeezed
   lemon juice
sea salt and freshly ground black
   pepper, to taste

GF, V+, DF

This potato salad is one of my barbecue favourites. It's creamy and satisfying, and the spring onions and dill add a wonderful texture that makes it irresistible. It keeps well, so any leftover salad can be used the next day. To make this a vegan salad, use Eggless Mayonnaise (p.79).

METHOD
Put the potatoes into a medium saucepan and cover with cold water. Bring to the boil, then turn down to a gentle simmer over a low heat and cook for about 15-20 minutes or until just tender (test by pushing a knife into one of the potatoes – if it slips off, then it's done). Drain in a colander and allow them to cool to room temperature.

To make the dressing, mix all the ingredients in a small bowl, seasoning with a small pinch of sea salt and black pepper to taste.

Put the cooled potatoes and chopped celery in a medium serving bowl and drizzle with the dressing. Mix until the potatoes are well coated. Chill the salad in fridge until ready to serve.

CHUCK IT IN CHEF'S SALAD

SERVES 4
Prep time: 15 minutes

INGREDIENTS
For the salad:

1 head baby gem lettuce, chopped
 into bite-sized pieces

70g watercress or rocket
 (large handful)

70g baby spinach leaves
 (large handful)

2 medium carrots, grated

2 spring onions, finely chopped

100g radishes, thinly sliced

For the dressing:

3 tablespoons extra-virgin olive oil

1½ teaspoons Dijon mustard

1 tablespoon white wine vinegar

I tablespoon freshly squeezed lemon
 juice (approx. ½ lemon)

small pinch sea salt and freshly
 ground black pepper, to taste

GF, V+, DF

As a child growing up in England with an American mother, I had a surprise one day after school when I went home to my best friend's house for dinner. Her mother offered me a salad, which I expected to be like one of my mum's, with lots of crunchy ingredients tossed together in a huge salad bowl and served with a delicious dressing. What I got was a single wedge of tomato, a lettuce leaf, a chunk of cucumber and some salad dressing poured over. It didn't quite have the wow factor of my mum's compositions. This salad is crisp, refreshing and the colours make it look as good as it tastes.

METHOD

Put all the prepared salad ingredients in large salad bowl. To make the dressing, whisk together all the ingredients in a small mixing bowl or mug.

Just before serving, drizzle the dressing over the salad and toss until evenly coated.

SWEET POTATO OVEN CHIPS

SERVES 1 (multiply the quantities below to serve more)
Prep time: 5 minutes
Cooking time: 30–35 minutes

INGREDIENTS
Per person:
1½ teaspoons vegetable oil or sunflower oil, plus more for greasing the trays
1 sweet potato
¼ teaspoon sea salt

GF, V+, DF

Sweet potatoes give a little sweet caramelised twist to the usual fries, and you have the added benefit of extra vitamin A and beta-carotene. And they're cooked in the oven to keep the fat content low. Tasty and good for you – what more could you ask for?

METHOD
Preheat the oven to 200°C/gas mark 6. Depending on how many people you are cooking for, coat the base of one or two baking trays lightly with a little oil.

Trim the ends off the potatoes. I leave the skin on, but peel now if preferred. Cut each sweet potato lengthways into medium-sized fries – around 1cm thick is perfect – or cut into wedges if you prefer. Just make sure they are all a similar size so that they will cook evenly. Put the fries in a mixing bowl, pour in the oil and sea salt and, using your hands, toss well until all the oil is evenly distributed.

Spread the uncooked fries evenly on the prepared trays, keeping them well spaced out. If they are overcrowded they tend to steam and become a bit soggy.

It's best to cook these fries on the top shelf of the oven, but if you have prepared enough for two baking trays, then put one on the middle shelf and one on the top. Swap the two trays around halfway through cooking. Turn the fries around a couple of times during baking to ensure they cook evenly.

Bake for 25-30 minutes, or until golden brown and turning crisp. Serve immediately.

SWEETCORN
WITH SAVOURY PARSLEY BUTTER

SERVES 4

Prep time: 10 minutes
Cooking time: 5 minutes

INGREDIENTS

4 ears of fresh sweetcorn

30g butter, margarine or coconut oil,
at room temperature

1 tablespoon chopped fresh parsley

1 tablespoon nutritional yeast flakes,
or 1 teaspoon Marmite

GF, V+, DF

I like to brush the savoury parsley butter onto hot, freshly cooked sweetcorn. The nutritional yeast is a good source of B vitamins and if you want to make this dish dairy-free, you can use a dairy-free spread instead of butter.

METHOD

If your sweetcorn is not already husked, then prepare it by pulling back the outer leaves to expose the ear of corn. Strip off any of the silky threads still clinging to the cob, then rinse under cold water.

To make the savoury butter, mix the butter (or oil), chopped parsley and nutritional yeast flakes (or Marmite) in a small bowl, using a fork.

To cook the sweetcorn, bring a large saucepan of water to the boil – use enough water so that the corn will be completely submerged. Once the water is boiling, carefully place the corn in the pan and cook for around 3–4 minutes. Then remove the corn from the pan and drain on kitchen paper to get rid of the excess water.

Place a ridged griddle pan over a medium-high heat until smoking hot. Add the corn and cook for a few minutes until charred, turning to cook on all sides. Or, you could do this on a BBQ instead.

While the corn is still hot, use a pastry brush to spread the softened butter mix evenly over it. Serve hot.

KEY LIME AND COCONUT PIE

SERVES 6–12 (6 very generous slices or 12 smaller slices)

Prep time: 15 minutes

Cooking time: 25–30 minutes

Cooling time: 20 minutes

Freezing/chilling time: 1 hour if freezing; 5 hours if chilling in fridge

INGREDIENTS

175g digestive biscuits

100g coconut oil or butter, melted

40g desiccated coconut

3 large eggs

397g tin condensed milk

juice of 5 limes (approx. 150ml)

zest of 1 lime

120ml coconut milk

GF

I grew up loving Key lime pie but wanted to give it a little twist, so I experimented by adding coconut. This pie has a coconut-infused biscuit crumb base, topped with a lime and coconut creamy filling. Key limes are famously grown in Florida, but this recipe works just as well with the usual variety of limes that are widely available. I sometimes use gluten-free biscuits to make this dessert gluten-free. Any leftovers can be left in the fridge.

METHOD

Preheat the oven to 170°C/gas mark 3. Get out a 23cm pie dish or loose-bottomed flan tin, about 3.5cm deep.

Blend the biscuits into rough crumbs in a food processor (or bash them with a rolling pin in a freezer bag). Then put the biscuits crumbs into a medium mixing bowl. Stir in the melted coconut oil or butter and the desiccated coconut. Press this biscuit mix into the base of your pie dish or flan tin and bake for 10 minutes.

Separate two of the eggs and put the egg yolks into a medium mixing bowl and the egg whites into a separate dry, clean medium bowl.

Add the third egg and the remaining ingredients to the bowl containing the egg yolks, and beat together well with a wooden spoon or hand whisk. Now, using a clean electric or hand whisk, whisk the egg whites to form soft firm peaks.

Gently fold the whisked egg whites into the coconut lime egg mixture so it is well combined. Pour this mixture evenly over the biscuit base and bake for 15-20 minutes, until set on top but still slightly wobbly in the centre.

Remove from the oven and leave to cool for 20 minutes. Then cover with cling film and either freeze for a minimum of 1 hour or chill in the fridge for 5 hours (or preferably overnight) before serving. This will keep in the fridge for up to 3 days.

I HEART MEXICAN

FOOD

I HEART MEXICAN FOOD

As a family, we grew up loving Mexican food. I think it was all about the assembly: when we were kids we loved putting together the prepared ingredients for a great taco or tostada ourselves, always a mouthwatering process. Healthy ingredients, vibrant colours and lots of variety make Mexican food a firm favourite for my family today.

MENU

Homemade Corn Tortillas - GF, V+, DF

Tostadas Deluxe - GF

Cornbread with Jalapeño and Sweetcorn

Mushroom and Cheese Quesadillas

Mexican Inspired Rice - GF, V+, DF

Avocado, Spring Onion and Lime - GF, V+, DF

Mixed Peppers - GF, V+, DF

Cucumber and Watermelon Salad - GF, V+, DF

Dad's Margarita - GF, V+, DF

Mango Granita - GF, V+, DF

HOMEMADE CORN TORTILLAS

MAKES 8 TORTILLAS

approx. 13cm in diameter

Prep time: 20 minutes

Resting time: 30 minutes

Cooking time: approx. 3 minutes per tortilla

INGREDIENTS

140g masa harina flour

180ml just boiled water

½ teaspoon sea salt

GF, V+, DF

Corn tortillas are made with masa harina flour (flour made from cooked corn kernels), which you can buy in specialist shops and online. Homemade corn tortillas may not look as perfectly shaped as their shop-bought cousins but I think they have so much more flavour, and using cornflour means these tortillas are gluten-free. Any leftovers can be wrapped up in foil and kept in the freezer until you need them. When it's time to use them, I give them a light sprinkle of water, then wrap in baking foil and heat in the oven.

METHOD

Put the flour into a medium mixing bowl. Gradually stir in the hot water with a wooden spoon. Then use your hands to knead the mixture together to form a ball. Wrap the dough in cling film and leave to rest in the fridge for 30 minutes.

Take the dough out of the fridge and cut it into eight equal pieces. Using your hands, roll each piece into a ball. Now take two sheets of greaseproof paper and sandwich one of the dough balls between them. Using a rolling pin, roll out the dough between the two sheets. Turn the tortilla 90 degrees clockwise then roll again, and keep turning and rolling until the tortilla is very thin, about 2mm. Repeat with the rest of the dough balls.

Place a medium to large, heavy-bottomed frying pan (no oil) over a medium-high heat. Once the pan is hot, place the corn tortillas in, two at a time if space allows. Cook them for 1½–2 minutes on one side, pressing down with a spatula if necessary to deflate any air bubbles that may form. Then flip them over with a spatula and cook on the other side for a further 1½–2 minutes, until cooked through. Stack the cooked tortillas on a plate as you go and cover with a clean tea towel (the tortillas will steam slightly and become softer and more pliable).

These are now ready to go. I use them for the Tostadas Deluxe (p.100).

TOSTADAS DELUXE

MAKES 4 TORTILLAS
(1 or 2 tortillas per person)
Prep time: 10 minutes
Cooking time: 5 minutes

INGREDIENTS

2 tablespoons light olive oil or
　vegetable oil
400g tin pinto or black beans, drained
1 medium clove garlic, finely chopped
½ teaspoon ground cumin
1 small or medium red onion,
　finely chopped
1 ripe tomato, finely chopped
1 tablespoon chopped jalapeño
1 avocado, halved, stoned, peeled
　and cut into small cubes
1 tablespoon finely chopped
　coriander or parsley
1 tablespoon freshly squeezed lime
　juice (approx. ½ lime)
1 teaspoon extra-virgin olive oil
4 ready-made corn or flour tortillas,
　approx. 13cm in diameter (shop-
　bought, or see recipe for Homemade
　Corn Tortillas on p.99)
100g goat's cheese or feta, crumbled
pinch sea salt, or to taste

GF

Corn tortillas topped with a chunky bean spread and then sprinkled with cheese, red onion, jalapeño, tomato, avocado and lime. Tostadas are a staple in my home because they're healthy, quick and easy to make and so satisfying. In a way, they have replaced toast as a base on which to build a great snack or light meal.

METHOD

Preheat the oven to 180°C/gas mark 4.

Heat the oil in a medium frying pan, add the beans and partially mash them with a fork or potato masher. Then add the garlic and ground cumin and fry for 5 minutes.

In a medium bowl, mix together the red onion, tomato, jalapeño, avocado, coriander or parsley and a small pinch of sea salt. Add the lime juice and extra-virgin olive oil and toss the ingredients together.

Heat the tortillas by wrapping them in foil and popping into the warm oven for around 5 minutes.

To assemble the tostadas, spread the bean mixture over the base of each heated tortilla, then spoon the salad mix over the top and finish with a crumbling of cheese.

CORNBREAD WITH JALAPEÑO AND SWEETCORN

MAKES 12 PIECES

Prep time: 15 minutes
Cooking time: 20 minutes

INGREDIENTS

30g cornmeal or fine polenta, plus
   more for dusting the tin
115g plain or spelt flour
2 teaspoons baking powder
½ teaspoon bicarbonate of soda
150ml milk
1 tablespoon runny honey
2 large eggs
150g plain whole milk yoghurt
25g butter, melted
2 tablespoons jalapeños, chopped
50g sweetcorn, cut fresh from the cob
   (or frozen and thawed, or tinned
   and drained)

I like a fresh warm batch of this cornbread in a basket to pick at with this Mexican menu, but I also love it served alongside the One-Pot Chilli on p.194. And sometimes I simply have it warm with a little butter spread on top for a great snack.

METHOD

Preheat the oven to 200°C/gas mark 6. Grease a 23 x 23cm baking tin and dust with cornmeal or polenta.

In a large bowl, mix the cornmeal (or polenta) with the plain (or spelt) flour, baking powder and bicarbonate of soda.

In a separate bowl, combine the milk, honey, eggs, yoghurt and melted butter. Gradually stir this mixture into the bowl of dry ingredients until thoroughly combined, but do not overmix.

Now stir in the jalapeños and sweetcorn. Immediately pour the batter into the baking tin and bake for about 20 minutes until golden brown.

Cut into 12 pieces and serve warm.

MUSHROOM AND CHEESE QUESADILLAS

SERVES 4
Prep time: 5 minutes
Cooking time: 12 minutes

INGREDIENTS
2 tablespoons light olive oil or
    vegetable oil
250g mushrooms, thinly sliced
2 cloves garlic, finely chopped
8 ready-made soft tortillas, approx.
    20cm in diameter (you can buy
    gluten-free)
200g mature Cheddar, grated
2 tablespoons finely chopped
    coriander or parsley
2 tablespoons jalapeños,
    roughly chopped

GF

*So quick to make and so moreish, these quesadillas (hot tortilla sandwiches)
also make a great lunch, served simply with a crisp green salad tossed in
a lemon and olive oil dressing.*

METHOD
Heat the oil in a medium frying pan over a medium-high heat. Add
the mushrooms and fry for 2 minutes, stirring often. Add the garlic
and fry for a further 2 minutes, until the mushrooms are browned
and the juices have evaporated.

Spoon the mushrooms evenly over four of the tortillas, then sprinkle
the cheese, herbs and jalapeños over the mushrooms and sandwich
each one with another tortilla on top.

Heat a clean, medium frying pan (no oil) over a medium-high heat,
then add the first quesadilla and cook for about 1–5 minutes, or until
lightly browned and crisp. Carefully flip the quesadilla over, using
a spatula, and cook on the other side until it's golden brown and
the cheese has gone nice and melty. Remove from the pan and set
aside to keep warm.

Repeat with the remaining quesadillas. Once they are all cooked, cut
each quesadilla into quarters.

Eat while hot.

MEXICAN-INSPIRED RICE

SERVES 4–6

Prep time: 10 minutes
Cooking time: approx. 25 minutes
(depending on rice cooking time)

INGREDIENTS

1 tablespoon light olive oil or
    vegetable oil
1 medium onion, finely chopped
3 cloves garlic, finely chopped
300g brown rice
800ml hot vegetable stock
4 ripe tomatoes, skinned and finely
    chopped (see p.65 for how to skin
    the tomatoes)
1 medium-hot red chilli, deseeded and
    finely chopped, or ½ teaspoon chilli
    flakes (optional)
2 tablespoons finely chopped fresh
    coriander or parsley, or 2 teaspoons
    dried herbs
1 lime, cut into 4 wedges

GF, V+, DF

This tomato- and onion-infused rice makes a really great side dish that sits happily alongside these Mexican recipes – although I'd gladly eat a bowlful on its own with some grated cheese and chopped parsley sprinkled on top!

METHOD

Heat the oil in a medium, heavy-bottomed saucepan, then add the onion and fry for 2 minutes. Stir in the garlic and the uncooked brown rice and cook through for 1 minute. Pour in the hot vegetable stock and mix in the tomatoes and the chopped red chilli (if using).

Cover and simmer gently until the stock has evaporated. This will take around 20-25 minutes (depending on the type of rice you use – check the packet for instructions). Test the rice, and add more stock if it's not ready yet.

Once the rice is cooked, turn off the heat, remove the lid and cover the pan with a clean, dry tea towel. Leave for about 5 minutes. This will absorb the steam and leave the rice fluffy and separated.

Mix in the coriander or parsley with a fork and serve with a lime wedge on each plate to squeeze over before eating.

AVOCADO, SPRING ONION AND LIME

SERVES 4

Prep time: 5 minutes

INGREDIENTS

2 ripe avocados (½ per person)
2 spring onions, finely chopped
2 limes, halved
pinch sea salt

GF, V+, DF

This is a very simple dish but the trick to making it really great is to use perfectly ripe avocados. I can't get enough of avocados and the extra bonus is just how healthy they are. They're a rich source of essential healthy fats. I'm always happy when being healthy involves eating more of something I love. It's the perfect accompaniment to the Tostadas Deluxe (p.100) and the Mushroom and Cheese Quesadillas (p.105).

Make sure the rest of your meal is ready to go before you serve this – the avocado will start to go brown if it's left hanging around.

METHOD

Cut the avocados in half lengthways and remove the stones. Using a metal dessertspoon, gently scoop out the flesh, keeping it intact. Slice the scooped-out avocado, sprinkle with the chopped spring onions, a squeeze of lime and a pinch of sea salt. Ready to serve.

MIXED PEPPERS

SERVES 4

Prep time: 5 minutes
Cooking time: 7 minutes

INGREDIENTS

1 red pepper
1 yellow pepper
1 orange or green pepper
1 tablespoon light olive oil
   or vegetable oil
juice of ½ lime
1 teaspoon chipotle paste
pinch sea salt, or to taste

GF, V+, DF

This is a wonderful, brightly coloured side dish. With the addition of the chipotle paste, the peppers take on a delicious smoked flavour. Chipotle paste is made from dried, smoked jalapeño peppers. If you don't have any you can use a pinch of chilli flakes instead.

METHOD

Remove the woody stem, core and seeds from the peppers and cut the flesh into 1cm strips.

Heat the oil in a large frying pan over a medium-high heat. Add the peppers and toss in the oil for 2 minutes. Add the lime juice and chipotle paste and toss around to coat the pepper strips evenly. Continue to cook over a medium-high heat for a further 5 minutes. Serve either hot or at room temperature.

CUCUMBER AND WATERMELON SALAD

SERVES 4–6
Prep time: 10 minutes

INGREDIENTS
For the dressing:
1 tablespoon extra-virgin olive oil
2 tablespoons lime juice
pinch sea salt

For the salad:
300g watermelon
½ cucumber (approx. 200g)
2 tablespoons pumpkin seeds
40g rocket (about a handful)

GF, V+, DF

The combination of watermelon and cucumber provides a juicy salad that, to me, symbolises summer on a plate. It's a great counterbalance to the slightly spicy food in the rest of this menu.

METHOD
Make your dressing first. In a cup or small bowl, whisk together the olive oil, lime juice and pinch of sea salt, using a fork.

For the salad, peel the watermelon and cut into 2cm chunks – remove the seeds if you like. Place in a sieve to allow any juices to drain away while you prepare the other ingredients.

Cut the cucumber into four lengthways and peel if desired. Then cut into 2cm cubes.

Toast the pumpkin seeds in a dry, heavy-bottomed frying pan for a few minutes until they crisp up, then turn off the heat and transfer to a small dish as soon as they start to colour. Be careful not to burn them.

Put the cubes of watermelon and cucumber into a large serving bowl, then drizzle the dressing over them and mix together. Finally, toss in the rocket and toasted pumpkin seeds just before serving.

DAD'S MARGARITA

SERVES 2

Prep time: 10 minutes

INGREDIENTS

1 lime, halved, for rubbing around
    the rim of the glass

finely ground sea salt, for lightly
    salting the rim of the glass

2 shots of tequila

2 shots of Cointreau, or 1 shot
    Cointreau and 1 shot triple sec

juice of 1 orange

juice of 3 limes

ice cubes

GF, V+, DF

This is my dad's recipe, which has been adopted by friends and family everywhere. It has a real kick to it, so please drink it responsibly. I have to say, Dad makes the best margarita I have ever tasted, full stop!

METHOD

To salt the rims of the glasses, run the half-cut lime around the rim of each glass. Fill a saucer with super-fine sea salt. Dab each glass lightly into the salt, turning it slowly so that the outer rim is covered (not the inside or it will make your cocktail too salty when you take a sip).

Mix the remaining ingredients (except the ice) in a cocktail shaker, adding the ice at the last minute, then shake vigorously, pour and enjoy!

MANGO GRANITA

SERVES 4
Prep time: 10 minutes
Freezing time: 3–6 hours or overnight

INGREDIENTS
3 ripe sweet mangoes, peeled and
   cut away from the stone
1 teaspoon finely grated lime zest
240ml water
1 tablespoon freshly squeezed lime
   juice (approx. ½ lime)
1 passion fruit, halved, for garnish

GF, V+, DF

This refreshing sorbet–like dessert requires the flesh of juicy, ripe mangoes and provides a tangy finish to this Mexican-inspired menu.

METHOD

Chop the mangoes roughly into chunky pieces and put in a food processor with the lime zest. Process until completely smooth - about 1-2 minutes - stopping the machine to scrape down the sides with a rubber spatula as needed. Transfer the purée to a medium bowl and add the water and lime juice. Stir with a large spoon to combine.

Pour the purée into a 20 x 20cm metal baking tray or any metal tray of a similar size that will fit into your freezer. (This size works best because it provides a large surface area, which helps speed up the freezing process.)

Put the purée into the freezer and stir every 30 minutes, being sure to scrape the ice crystals off the sides and into the middle of the pan, until the mixture is too frozen to stir - this should be about 3 hours, depending on how cold your freezer is. Use a large dinner fork to stir and scrape and break up the ice crystals.

When you're ready to serve the granita, scoop it into chilled glasses or bowls (if it has been in the freezer overnight, you may need to take it out 10 minutes beforehand to allow it to soften slightly). I like to spoon a few passion fruit seeds on top of each serving.

AFTERNOON
....
TEA PARTY

AFTERNOON TEA PARTY

For 12

The afternoon tea party is a tradition going back years: sipping on tea, snacking on sandwiches and cakes and biscuits and chit-chatting the afternoon away. What could possibly be better? You can use any number of excuses – celebrating the arrival of a special guest, a birthday, a baby shower, or just getting friends over for a treat. For the food, I like a balance between a selection of savoury and sweet treats, freshly prepared sandwiches cut into bite-sized pieces, plates of biscuits and a centrepiece loaf cake that my guests can help themselves to throughout the afternoon.

MENU

Sandwich Selection

Fava Bean Dip - GF, V+, DF

Coconut Loaf Cake

Moist Carrot and Apple Madeleines - DF

White Chocolate Chunk Cookies - GF, DF

Florentines - GF, V+, DF

Peanut Butter Cookies - GF, DF

SANDWICH SELECTION
CHOOSE 2 OR 3 COMBINATIONS PER TEA PARTY

I think I could live on sandwiches! I like to make a variety, both closed and open-faced, and I have suggested a couple of options using oatcakes or crackers for a change. You can keep it simple by using just one type of sandwich bread and serve it several different ways, or experiment with a variety of breads from seeded to gluten-free. Traditionally, you would trim off the crusts of the sandwiches for a tea party – if you choose to do this you can reuse the crusts by blitzing them in a food processor and then storing them as breadcrumbs to cook with at a later date. (Any of these suggestions can be gluten-free if you use gluten-free bread or oatcakes.)

Sliced Boiled Egg with Mayonnaise and Chopped Watercress with a squeeze of fresh lemon juice and a sprinkle of sea salt (see p.79 for Eggless Mayonnaise recipe) - GF, DF

Smoked Applewood Cheddar with Red Cabbage and Grated Apple Coleslaw (for the coleslaw, grate some red cabbage and apple, then mix with mayonnaise and a squeeze of fresh lemon juice), or smoked applewood cheddar with sliced peach - GF

Half-fat Crème Fraîche, Roasted Red Pimento Pepper and Chives on an oatcake or buckwheat cracker - GF

Peanut Butter and Raspberry Jam on an oatcake or buckwheat cracker - GF, V+, DF

Chopped Banana with Honey and Cream Cheese - GF

Emmental Cheese, Dijon Mustard, Sliced Cucumber Pickle and Sauerkraut - GF

Oven-Roasted Red Onions with Goat's Cheese, Chilli Jam and Crisp Lettuce - GF

Hummous and Thinly Sliced Cucumber, or hummous with sliced pickled beetroot (see p.54 for Hummous recipe) - GF, V+, DF

FAVA BEAN DIP

SERVES 4–6

Prep time: 10 minutes (if using podded broad beans); 20 minutes (if removing the outer skin)

Cooking time: 5 minutes

INGREDIENTS

500g podded broad beans, or 750g frozen broad beans in their skins (most supermarkets or specialist shops sell these), defrosted

2 spring onions, thinly sliced

2 teaspoons vegetable bouillon powder

zest and juice of ½ lemon

3 tablespoons extra-virgin olive oil

2 tablespoons mayonnaise

½ tablespoon finely chopped fresh mint

½ tablespoon finely chopped fresh basil

½ teaspoon chilli flakes (optional)

GF, V+, DF

Fava beans (broad beans) are a delicious and often overlooked ingredient and if you fancy a change from hummous, they make a fabulous vibrant green dip that's great served with vegetable sticks or on little gem lettuce leaves or spread on to oatcakes or other crackers with thinly sliced radish. For a vegan option, use Eggless Mayonnaise (p.79).

METHOD

If using frozen broad beans in their skins, place the beans in hot water for 2 minutes, then gently squeeze out the vibrant green beans from their skins.

Place the beans in a medium saucepan with the spring onions, bouillon powder and just enough water to cover the beans.

Bring to the boil and then lower the heat to a gentle simmer. Cook for 2 minutes, then remove from the heat. Do not drain. Reserve a few beans for the garnish, then add all the other ingredients to the pan and blitz with a stick blender or in a food processor (or you can just mash with a potato masher).

Add a little extra water if the mix is too thick. Chill the dip and when you are ready to serve, garnish with the reserved beans.

COCONUT LOAF CAKE

SERVES 10–12

Prep time: 20 minutes
Cooking time: 50 minutes

INGREDIENTS

For the sponge:

280g plain or spelt flour
1½ teaspoons baking powder
150g desiccated coconut
zest of ½ lemon
240g sugar
2 large eggs
2 teaspoons vanilla extract
80g butter, melted, plus more for
    greasing the tin
200ml coconut milk

For the icing:

100g icing sugar, sifted
1½ tablespoons water

For decoration (optional):

50g coconut flakes

This loaf cake, flavoured with a hint of coconut, brings a little glamour to the table. It's easy to make, fluffy and delicious. It makes a pretty centrepiece to a tea party with the white icing dripping down the sides.

METHOD

Preheat the oven to 180°C/gas mark 4. Grease and line a 23 x 13cm loaf tin.

Sift the flour and baking powder into a large mixing bowl, then add the desiccated coconut and lemon zest.

In a medium bowl, beat the sugar and eggs together, then stir in the vanilla extract, melted butter and coconut milk.

Make a well in the centre of your flour mixture and then gradually pour in the coconut milk and egg mix, stirring until it's well combined with the dry ingredients. Now pour the batter into the prepared loaf tin.

Bake for 50 minutes, then check by inserting a skewer into the centre of the cake. If it comes out clean the cake is done – if not, put it back in the oven for another 5 minutes and then check again.

Turn the cake out of the tin on to a wire rack or plate and allow it to come to room temperature before icing.

While the cake is cooling, mix the sifted icing sugar with the water in a bowl and beat until smooth. The icing needs to be thick enough to coat the back of a spoon. If it's too thin, add a little more sifted icing sugar; if it's too thick, add a few more drops of water. Remember to do it little by little.

Pour the icing over the cake evenly, making sure you cover the entire surface and letting it drizzle down the sides. While it is still wet, scatter with coconut flakes (if using) and serve.

MOIST CARROT AND
APPLE MADELEINES

MAKES 6

Prep time: 15 minutes
Cooking time: 15 minutes

INGREDIENTS

90g plain or spelt flour
½ teaspoon baking powder
¼ teaspoon ground cinnamon
¼ teaspoon bicarbonate of soda
¼ teaspoon salt
1 medium egg, lightly beaten
50g soft light brown sugar or
    coconut sugar
30g vegetable oil, plus more for
    greasing the tin
1 medium carrot (approx. 70g), grated
½ apple, peeled and grated
icing sugar, for sprinkling
    on top (optional)

DF

Madeleines are tradition small cakes from northeastern France. They are baked in a tray of small cake moulds shaped like shells. If you don't have a madeleine tray, you can bake them in small cupcake cases in a cupcake tin instead (just don't serve the madeleines in the cases). The addition of grated carrot and apple gives these cakes extra texture and bite.

METHOD

Preheat the oven to 180°C/gas mark 4. Lightly grease a metal or silicone madeleine tray (or use small cupcake cases in a cupcake tin).

Sift the flour, baking powder, cinnamon, bicarbonate of soda and salt into a medium bowl and stir to combine.

In a separate, larger bowl, whisk together the egg and sugar until fluffy, then stir in the vegetable oil and grated carrot and apple.

Add the dry ingredients to the wet ingredients, stirring until just blended. Spoon the madeleine mixture into the prepared tray and bake for about 15 minutes (or until cooked through the tops of the madeleines should spring back when touched).

Remove from the oven and leave to cool slightly in their tray, then gently remove each madeleine from the tray and lay on to a wire rack to cool. Dust with icing sugar just before serving for a pretty finishing touch.

These will keep for 2–3 days in an airtight container.

WHITE CHOCOLATE CHUNK COOKIES

MAKES APPROX. 18 COOKIES
Prep time: 10 minutes
Cooking time: 8 minutes

INGREDIENTS

100g butter (or coconut oil for dairy-free option), plus more for greasing the trays

110g coconut sugar or granulated sugar

1 large egg

1 tablespoon cocoa powder

150g buckwheat flour (for gluten-free option) or plain or spelt flour

100g white chocolate, broken into small pieces

GF, DF

I like to make a batch of cookies to keep in a cookie jar, ready to offer to friends when they come over for tea, and I love to see the kids arrive home and head straight for the jar. I usually make these gluten-free and use coconut sugar and coconut oil, because they are delicious and it makes me feel less guilty when I eat three in a row!

METHOD

Preheat the oven to 180°C/gas mark 4 and lightly grease two baking trays.

Cream together the butter (or oil) and sugar in a large bowl until light and creamy. Beat in the egg, cocoa powder and flour until all the ingredients are well combined. Stir in the white chocolate pieces, making sure they are distributed evenly throughout the mixture.

Drop teaspoonfuls of the cookie dough onto the prepared baking trays, leaving a 4cm gap between each cookie to allow room for them to spread during baking. Flatten them slightly with the back of a fork.

Bake for 8 minutes (do not overbake – they will seem a bit underdone but will set nicely on cooling). Use a spatula to ease the cookies off the baking trays on to a plate and leave to cool before eating.

These cookies will keep for up to 5 days in an airtight container.

FLORENTINES

MAKES 20

Prep time: 15 minutes

Cooking time: 10 minutes per batch

INGREDIENTS

vegetable oil, for greasing the trays

45g butter (or coconut butter for
   dairy-free option)

75g caster sugar

2 tablespoons buckwheat flour (for
   gluten-free option) or plain or
   spelt flour

2 tablespoons single cream (or soya
   cream for dairy-free option)

50g almonds, roughly chopped, or
   flaked almonds

30g shelled pistachios, chopped

zest of 1 lemon

zest of ½ orange

50g dried cranberries,
   roughly chopped

150g dark chocolate (minimum 70%
   cocoa solids), broken into chunks

GF, V+, DF

My second son got me into Florentines. They're sweet, nutty, fruity, zesty – and they have chocolate too! The perfect sweet treat.

METHOD

Preheat the oven to 180°C/gas mark 4. Lightly grease two baking trays with vegetable oil. (Alternatively, you can use one baking tray and cook the florentines in two batches.)

Warm the butter, sugar and flour in a small saucepan over a medium heat, stirring often, until the butter has melted. Remove from the heat, allow to cool slightly and gradually add the cream, stirring well until combined. Add the almonds, pistachios, lemon and orange zest and cranberries and mix well until everything is thoroughly combined. Drop 1 heaped teaspoonful of the florentine mixture at a time on the prepared baking trays, leaving a 3cm gap between each one so they don't merge together during baking. Press them down a little with the back of the spoon to flatten.

Bake the florentines for 10 minutes, or until golden brown. Remove from the oven and set aside to cool on their trays for a couple of minutes. Then carefully lift them off with a palette knife and transfer to a wire cooling rack or plate.

Melt the chocolate chunks in a heatproof bowl suspended over a pan of simmering water (not letting the bowl touch the water). Stir until smooth and melted.

When the florentines are completely cool, flip them over so that the flat base is facing upwards. Spread the melted chocolate lightly and evenly over the bases and set aside to cool and set. If you are not serving these straight away, you can store the florentines in layers between sheets of greaseproof paper in an airtight container for up to 5 days.

PEANUT BUTTER COOKIES

MAKES APPROX. 24 COOKIES

Prep time: 10 minutes
Cooking time: 8 minutes

INGREDIENTS

140g butter (or coconut oil for
    dairy-free option)
100g coconut sugar or
    granulated sugar
1 large egg
7 tablespoons crunchy peanut butter
130g buckwheat flour (for gluten-free
    option) or plain or spelt flour

GF, DF

My eldest son first made these cookies for me last summer. As I've been eating less and less gluten recently, he adapted his recipe to make it gluten-free. Once a batch of these cookies is made they do not stick around for long. I now keep a supply of coconut sugar in my store cupboard because it has a sweet caramel flavour and is a good source of minerals (it's available in specialist shops and most supermarkets).

METHOD

Preheat the oven to 180°C/gas mark 4. Line two baking trays with greaseproof paper.

Cream together the butter (or oil) and sugar in a large bowl until light and creamy. Beat in the egg and crunchy peanut butter. Finally, mix in the flour until all the ingredients are well combined.

Take 1 heaped teaspoon of the mixture at a time and place them on the baking trays about 3cm apart, to allow for any spread during baking. You should have about 24 small balls of cookie dough. Flatten them slightly with the back of a fork.

Bake the cookies for 8–9 minutes until golden brown. Then ease them off the baking trays and on to a plate to cool. These cookies will keep for up to 5 days in an airtight container.

DINNER

FOR TWO

DINNER FOR TWO

For 2

There are people in your life that you want to make time for, whether it's a best friend, a family member or your partner. Taking the time to make a special meal for that someone means you can really concentrate on turning it into an occasion and show how much you care. I always find people are more relaxed and the conversation flows much better if it's over good food… and wine. Although all of the recipes in this menu are for two, they can very easily be doubled, or trebled, if you're cooking for more.

MENU

Warm Mushroom Salad - GF, V+, DF

Individual White Onion and Tarragon Tarts - GF

Green Beans with Sesame Seeds and Lemon - GF, V+, DF

Individual Chocolate Almond Tortes - GF, DF

WARM MUSHROOM SALAD

SERVES 2
Prep time: 10 minutes
Cooking time: 15 minutes

INGREDIENTS

4 new potatoes, chopped into bite-
    sized cubes
1½ tablespoons light olive oil
250g mixed mushrooms (e.g. shitake,
    oyster, chestnut mushrooms), sliced
1 clove garlic, finely chopped
1 teaspoon fresh thyme leaves,
    woody stalks removed
1 teaspoon tamari (for gluten-free
    option) or soy sauce
2 teaspoons freshly squeezed
    lemon juice
80g mixed salad leaves (approx.
    2 handfuls)

For the dressing:

2 teaspoons extra-virgin olive oil
squeeze of fresh lemon juice
    (1 teaspoon)
sea salt and freshly ground black
    pepper, to taste

GF, V+, DF

This combination of warm sautéed mushrooms tossed in a tangy salad dressing and then piled on top of new potatoes and fresh dressed salad leaves is a really satisfying first course. Makes the perfect quick lunch, too.

METHOD

Place the bite-sized new potatoes in a pan of water and bring to the boil. Simmer gently for 10 minutes, or until just tender. Drain, then set aside to cool.

Heat the olive oil in a medium frying pan over a medium heat. Add the sliced mushrooms and chopped garlic and sauté for about 5 minutes, or until just beginning to brown. Add the fresh thyme and stir gently. Turn off the heat. Now stir in the tamari or soy sauce and the lemon juice.

When ready to serve, dress the salad leaves. Place the leaves in a medium bowl along with the cooled new potatoes, then drizzle with the olive oil, a squeeze of fresh lemon juice, a sprinkle of sea salt and black pepper, and toss together. Divide between two serving plates and heap the mushrooms on top.

INDIVIDUAL WHITE ONION AND TARRAGON TARTS

SERVES 2

Prep time: 30 minutes

Chilling time: 20 minutes

Cooking time: 35 minutes

INGREDIENTS

For the pastry:

100g plain or spelt flour, plus more for dusting the tin and worktop

50g salted butter, chilled and cut into cubes (keep the cubes in the fridge until you need them), plus more for greasing the tin

1 tablespoon iced water

1 egg, beaten, or a little milk, for brushing on the pastry

For the filling:

1 tablespoon light olive oil

100g white onions (approx. 2 medium), halved and thinly sliced

75g shallots (approx. 3 medium), roughly chopped

4 tablespoons white wine

15g butter

1 tablespoon plain, buckwheat or spelt flour

150ml milk

1 teaspoon wholegrain mustard

1 tablespoon finely chopped fresh tarragon

sea salt and freshly ground black pepper, to taste

GF

I love the flavour combination of the onions and shallots encased within this comforting white wine, fresh tarragon and wholegrain mustard sauce. These indulgent and warming tarts are easy to make, but they look – and taste – so good. You can make the pastry in advance, as it keeps chilled in the fridge for up to 5 days. Just take it out 10 minutes before rolling to allow it to reach room temperature. And of course, if you're short on time, you can use shop-bought shortcrust pastry instead (and you can get gluten-free pastry).

METHOD

First, make the pastry. If using a food processor, put the flour and butter in the processor bowl and pulse until it resembles bread-crumbs. Pour in the chilled water and mix again until the dough just comes together into a ball. Wrap the ball in cling film and leave to chill in the fridge for at least 20 minutes. Take it out 10–15 minutes before you are ready to use it (depending on how warm your kitchen is).

If mixing by hand, make sure you don't let the butter get too warm and overworked; the less you handle it with warm hands the better. Place the flour in a mixing bowl and add the cold cubes of butter. Using your fingertips, gently blend the butter into the flour until you have formed crumbs, leaving some larger pea-sized clumps too. Add the water and, using a metal spoon, mix to bring the mixture together into a soft ball of dough. Wrap it in cling film and chill in the fridge as above.

To make the individual pastry cases, turn over a metal muffin tin, then grease the underside of two muffin cups with butter and dust with flour (so the pastry won't stick later), leaving at least one cup space between them to allow for easy removal of the pastry cases when cooked. Lightly dust a clean worktop with flour. Cut your dough into two equal portions and roll each one into a ball shape. Gently roll out the first pastry ball, turning it 45 degrees each time you roll to ensure the pastry doesn't split. Continue to roll and turn until the pastry is about 3mm thick. Repeat with the second portion of pastry. Gently lift the pastry circles and place over the greased upturned muffin tin, then carefully shape them to fit the upturned mounds. Trim away any excess pastry with scissors or a sharp knife. Place the tin in the fridge to chill for 10 minutes – this will stop the pastry cases from shrinking as they bake. Preheat the oven to 200°C/gas mark 6.

Brush the outer shell of the pastry cases with the egg or milk and place in the middle of the oven for 10–12 minutes, or until they start to turn a light golden colour. Remove from the oven and allow to cool for a few minutes, then carefully ease the pastry cases off the tin and place, bottom-down, on a baking tray – the right way up now! Put them back in the oven for a further 5–7 minutes until lightly crisp, then remove and set to one side while you make the filling.

Turn the oven down to 180°C/gas mark 4. To make the filling, warm the olive oil in a small frying pan over a medium heat. Add the onions and shallots and sauté gently for 2 minutes. Pour in the wine and allow to sizzle in the pan, stirring occasionally, for 8–10 minutes, until the onions have softened and are just starting to turn brown.

In the meantime, melt the butter in a small saucepan over a low heat, mix in the flour and heat through until you have formed a paste. Take off the heat and mix in the milk a little at a time, using a whisk in order to avoid the sauce becoming lumpy. Place back over a medium heat and stir often with a whisk for 2–4 minutes until you have a smooth, thick sauce.

Stir in the mustard, chopped tarragon and the onion mixture, then season with a pinch of sea salt and grind of black pepper to taste. Scoop the mixture generously into the two pastry cases.

Pop the tarts back into the oven for 8–9 minutes, until they are hot all the way through.

GREEN BEANS WITH SESAME SEEDS AND LEMON

SERVES 2

Prep time: 5 minutes

Cooking time: 5 minutes

INGREDIENTS

200g fine green beans, trimmed

1 teaspoon sesame seeds

5g butter, or 1 teaspoon extra-virgin
    olive oil

squeeze of fresh lemon juice (approx.
    1 teaspoon)

sea salt and freshly ground black
    pepper, to taste

GF, V+, DF

A very simple side dish that is crisp, flavourful and super-healthy. Green beans are a great source of protein, vitamins K, A and C and manganese and are high in dietary fibre.

METHOD

Bring a medium saucepan of water to the boil. Place the beans in a colander or steamer above the water, cover with a lid and steam until tender - about 3-5 minutes.

Meanwhile, heat a small or medium frying pan over a medium heat and toast the sesame seeds until lightly golden, this should only take a minute or two. Tip them out on to a saucer quickly to prevent burning.

Now, in the same frying pan, heat the butter or olive oil over a low heat, add the green beans and sesame seeds and squeeze a little lemon juice over them.

Transfer the cooked beans to a serving bowl and season with salt and freshly ground pepper. Serve immediately with the Individual White Onion and Tarragon Tarts (p.148).

These beans work just as well served at room temperature, as a salad.

INDIVIDUAL CHOCOLATE ALMOND TORTES

SERVES 2

Prep time: 15 minutes

Cooking time: 12 minutes

INGREDIENTS

100g salted butter or coconut oil, plus more for greasing the ramekins

cocoa powder, for dusting the ramekins

100g dark chocolate (minimum 70% cocoa solids), broken into even-sized chunks

2 large eggs, separated

40g ground almonds or pistachios (can be ground in food processor)

40g caster sugar

2 ramekins

GF, DF

The pairing of bitter dark chocolate with smooth ground almonds is seductive. When you bite into the centre of a torte, you get a soft, melting and delicious mouthful. By using ground almonds instead of flour, you have a gluten-free dessert that is easy to make but never fails to impress. The tortes can be kept unbaked in the fridge for 1–2 days, or frozen for up to 3 months. If frozen, allow 30 minutes to defrost before baking.

METHOD

Preheat the oven to 180°C/gas mark 4. Grease two ramekins with butter and dust with cocoa powder. Melt the 100g of butter and dark chocolate together by warming the butter in a small pan over a very low heat and then adding the chocolate chunks, stirring often, until the chocolate has just dissolved. Make sure the melting chocolate doesn't cook for too long; if it overheats it will go grainy instead of smooth. Take off the heat and transfer the chocolate sauce to a medium mixing bowl. Allow it to cool slightly for about 5 minutes.

Mix the egg yolks into the cooled chocolate mixture. Add the ground almonds and sugar and beat together. Then, in a separate, clean bowl, whisk the egg whites with a clean whisk until they form soft peaks. Gently fold the whisked egg whites into the chocolate mix.

Divide the chocolate mixture evenly between the ramekins and bake for 12 minutes, until the tops are just springy to the touch. You want the centres to be gooey, so be careful not to overcook them. Wearing oven gloves to protect your hands, remove the ramekins from the oven and gently tip them upside down to pop the tortes out onto your serving dish.

You can eat these tortes as they are, but I love them with a few fresh raspberries or strawberries and a spoonful of vanilla ice cream or cream.

KIDS'

MENU

KIDS' MENU

Let's face it, cooking for kids can be fairly ungratifying at times. You put all that thought and energy into making them nutritious meals just so you can get comments like, 'how many bites do I have to have?' The kids know when I'm trying to get 'healthy' food into them and just shut up shop.

To make life easier, and in the hope of some enthusiastic feedback, I've designed some simple, one-stop-shop meals for my kids and their friends that I know they like, and then I can sneak in some of the things that are good for them too. They're happy – and so am I. Phew!

MENU

Alphabet Soup - GF, V+, DF

Super Mac 'n' Cheese - GF

All-in-One Burrito - GF V+, DF

Fruit Chunks and Chocolate Dippy Sauce - GF

Let Them Have It Fruit Popsicles - GF, V+, DF

ALPHABET SOUP

SERVES 6

Prep time: 15 minutes
Cooking time: 30 minutes

INGREDIENTS

2 tablespoons light olive oil or
    vegetable oil
1 medium onion, finely chopped
1 stick celery, finely chopped
1 carrot, finely chopped
80g green beans, topped and tailed
    and finely chopped, or broccoli
    florets finely chopped
400g tin chopped tomatoes
1 teaspoon mixed dried herbs
400g tin cannellini beans, drained
700ml vegetable stock
1 bay leaf
60g mini alphabet-shaped pasta
    (or gluten-free small pasta)

GF, V+, DF

By using tiny pasta shaped as letters (bought from specialist Italian delis or supermarkets) I can produce a soup that my kids find entertaining as well as tasty. The letters make it fun to eat, and it has a great assortment of vegetables and small white beans for protein and extra texture. I often serve this with toast spread with hummous for them to dunk in. If you can't find tiny alphabet pasta, you can use small macaroni instead, or spaghetti broken up into small pieces.

METHOD

Heat the oil in a medium to large saucepan over a medium heat, then add the chopped onion, celery, carrot and green beans (or broccoli). Gently sauté for 5 minutes, before stirring in the chopped tomatoes and mixed herbs.

Bring to a bubble and then reduce the heat and simmer gently for 10 minutes. Now stir in the cannellini beans, vegetable stock and bay leaf. Bring the soup back to a simmer, cover and cook for a further 15 minutes.

Meanwhile, in a separate, small saucepan, cook the pasta as per the packet instructions, and drain.

Stir the cooked pasta into the soup. Remember to fish out the bay leaf just before you serve the soup.

SUPER MAC 'N' CHEESE

Prep time: 15 minutes
Cooking time: 20–25 minutes

INGREDIENTS

200g macaroni (or rice and corn
   pasta macaroni for gluten-
   free option)
½ head cauliflower (approx 250g),
   broken into small florets
2 tablespoons light olive oil or
   vegetable oil or butter
3 tablespoons buckwheat flour (for
   gluten-free option) or plain or
   spelt flour
500ml milk
1 teaspoon Dijon mustard
200g mature Cheddar, grated
100g frozen peas
2 tablespoons grated vegetarian
   Parmesan-style cheese, or similar
   vegetarian hard cheese
freshly ground black pepper,
   to taste (optional)

GF

This is a classic mac 'n' cheese, with small cauliflower florets and peas (both powerhouses of nutrition) mixed in. The kids love it and I am happy because they get two extra vegetables snuck in.

METHOD

Preheat the oven to 180°C/gas mark 4. You will need a 20 x 20cm ovenproof dish (or similar-sized dish) for this recipe.

Fill a medium saucepan with water, bring the water to the boil and add your pasta. Cook until just cooked through (al dente), checking the cooking time for your pasta on the packet. Drain, rinse under cold water and set aside.

Take the small cauliflower florets and steam over a steamer for about 7 minutes, or until just cooked through. Alternatively place in a medium saucepan of boiling water for about 6 minutes.

Drain the cauliflower in a sieve and run under cold water to stop it cooking. Set aside while you make the cheese sauce.

To make the cheese sauce, gently heat the oil (or butter) in a medium to large saucepan, then mix in the flour and stir with a wooden spoon until it forms a soft paste. Remove from the heat and gradually stir in the milk, using a wooden spoon or hand whisk, to prevent lumps forming.

Put the sauce back onto the heat and bring to a gentle bubble, stirring continuously until the sauce thickens, about 2–3 minutes. Turn off the heat and stir in the mustard and Cheddar. Now add the frozen peas and then gently mix in the cooked pasta and cauliflower. Add a little pepper if desired (you may not need salt as the cheese is quite salty). Spoon the mixture evenly into the ovenproof dish.

Sprinkle with the Parmesan-style cheese and bake for 15 minutes, or until the sauce bubbles and is golden brown on top.

ALL-IN-ONE BURRITO

SERVES 6
Prep time: 15 minutes
Cooking time: 20–25 minutes

INGREDIENTS

200g brown rice
2 tablespoons light olive oil or
   vegetable oil
1 medium onion, finely chopped
1 clove garlic, finely chopped
400g tin kidney beans, drained
400g tin chopped tomatoes
1 teaspoon agave syrup or
   runny honey
50g green beans, trimmed and
   chopped small
50g sweetcorn, cut fresh from the cob
   (or frozen and defrosted, or tinned
   and drained)
2 teaspoons dried mixed herbs or
   1 tablespoon chopped fresh parsley
6 ready-made soft corn or
   flour tortillas
80g Cheddar (or non-dairy
   cheese), grated

GF, V+, DF

The trick here is not to overstuff the tortillas, as they need to be tightly wrapped around the filling so that your kids can eat them with their hands. They are fun to eat and packed with healthy ingredients: a great source of fibre and protein, while the kidney beans provide iron too.

METHOD

Cook the rice in a saucepan of boiling water, following the instructions on the packet. I usually do one part rice to two parts boiled water, then cover with a lid and simmer for 20-25 minutes until the rice is cooked. Do not stir it while it is cooking. Test a bite and, if it is not quite ready, add a little more boiled water as required. Then turn off the heat, remove the lid and cover the pan with a clean tea towel to absorb the steam so you don't end up with stodgy rice.

While the rice is cooking you can get on with making the tomato sauce. Heat the oil in a medium-large frying pan over a medium-high heat. Sauté the onion for 7 minutes, then stir in the garlic and drained kidney beans. Carry on cooking for a couple of minutes, then stir in the tinned tomatoes and agave syrup or honey. Simmer gently for 10 minutes, then stir in the green beans, sweetcorn and mixed herbs and simmer for a further 10 minutes.

When the rice is ready, mix into the tomato sauce. Preheat the oven to 170°C/gas mark 3.

Wrap the tortillas in foil and warm them through in the oven for 5 minutes. Carefully remove the foil and put the tortillas on to plates. Spoon a couple of spoonfuls of the rice and tomato mix on to the middle of each tortilla, followed by a sprinkle of grated cheese, making sure that you don't overfill them as you need to leave room to wrap the tortillas tightly around the filling. Taking one tortilla at a time, fold the bottom of the tortilla up towards the centre, then fold in one side at a time to form a tortilla wrap. Now pick it up and take a bite!

FRUIT CHUNKS AND CHOCOLATE DIPPY SAUCE

SERVES 4
Prep time: 10 minutes
Cooking time: 5 minutes

INGREDIENTS

For the chocolate sauce:
100g milk chocolate (I like Green & Black's)
6 tablespoons milk

Fruit of your choice, such as:
2 kiwi fruits, peeled and cut into 4
1 banana, peeled and sliced into chunks
8 strawberries, hulled and cut in half
1 ripe mango, peeled and cut into bite-sized cubes
blueberries
pineapple chunks

GF

Easy to make, bright, colourful – and it's a joy to watch children eating this.

METHOD
Break the chocolate into pieces and place in a small saucepan along with the milk. Put the pan over a low heat and keep stirring until all the chocolate has just melted and you have a glossy sauce, then take off the heat. Be careful not to overheat the chocolate or it will burn and take on a gritty texture.

Prepare a selection of your child's favourite fruit. You can either thread the fruit on to wooden skewers or put it into a bowl and use forks.

Pour the chocolate sauce into one bowl to share, or into eggcups for individual portions (my kids love doing it this way). Ready to eat!

LET THEM HAVE IT
FRUIT POPSICLES

MAKES 8 POPSICLES
(of four different flavours)
Prep time: 15 minutes
Freezing time: Overnight

INGREDIENTS

8 strawberries, plus 3 tablespoons
    apple juice
12 raspberries, plus 2 tablespoons
    apple juice
1 ripe mango and 1 banana, plus
    3 tablespoons orange juice
1 ripe banana and 1 ripe peach, plus
    3 tablespoons apple juice

popsicle moulds or small paper cups
8 lollipop sticks or teaspoons

GF, V+, DF

I get the kids involved in making these. That way, they can have input in the flavour combinations they like best and we can experiment. These popsicles are a perfect summery treat, and kids of all ages love making them – including me. Each fruit combination below makes two popsicles, or you can quadruple the quantities in your favourite fruit combination to make eight of the same flavour.

METHOD

Prepare the fruit: hull the strawberries; peel the mango and remove the stone, then chop into chunks; peel and chop the banana; remove the stone from the peach and chop into chunks.

Whizz each of your chosen fruit and juice combinations in a blender, or with a stick blender in a jug, until smooth. Pour into popsicle moulds or small paper cups, insert a stick or teaspoon into each one so it stands upright, and freeze overnight or until frozen through.

BE PREPARED

DINNER PARTY

BE PREPARED DINNER PARTY

I enjoy having friends over for dinner and a catch-up. I want to cook something that will impress them but still be able to enjoy myself and not be so busy in the kitchen that I miss out on the latest laughs and news. So this menu is designed around recipes that you can prepare in advance and then just heat up or finish off easily when your guests arrive.

MENU

Super Pea and Watercress Soup with Grilled Cheese Croutons - GF, V+, DF

Courgette and Leek Fritters with Feta Citrus Dressing - GF

Herb and Cheese Soufflé - GF

Wilted Spinach - GF, V+, DF

Baked Plums with Fresh Basil and Amaretti Crisp - GF, V+, DF

SUPER PEA AND WATERCRESS SOUP
WITH GRILLED CHEESE CROUTONS

SERVES 6

Prep time: 10 minutes
Cooking time: 25 minutes

INGREDIENTS

For the soup:

2 tablespoons light olive oil or
    vegetable oil

2 medium white onions,
    roughly chopped

2 cloves garlic, roughly chopped

1 medium potato, roughly chopped

1 teaspoon dried mixed herbs

1 litre vegetable stock

400g peas (fresh or frozen)

75g watercress, washed

pinch sea salt and freshly ground
    black pepper, to taste

For the cheese croutons:

2 slices wholemeal sandwich bread,
    or other sliced bread of your choice

butter (or non-dairy alternative) for
    spreading on the bread

120g grated or sliced mature Cheddar
    or goat's Cheddar (or non-dairy
    cheese slice)

GF, V+, DF

This is a gorgeous, vibrant green soup. The peas add a subtle sweetness and the watercress a fresh peppery, mustardy taste. Watercress is my favourite leaf and I try to eat it every day. It's a superfood packed with nutrients such as vitamins A, C and K and is a good source of iron and antioxidants. The little grilled cheese croutons sprinkled on top of this soup add the perfect finishing touch. This dish is ideal as a dinner-party first course – you can make the soup the day before and keep it in the fridge, then all you have to do is prepare the croutons just before you serve the soup. It's great for lunch, too.

METHOD

Heat the oil in a large saucepan over a medium heat and sauté the onions, garlic and potato for 4 minutes. Stir in the mixed herbs and vegetable stock, bring to the boil, then turn down the heat and simmer gently for 10 minutes. Add the peas to the pan, bring back up to a gentle simmer and cook for a further 10 minutes, then turn off the heat.

Stir in the watercress, then whizz with a stick blender to create a vibrant green, smooth soup. (Or you can leave to cool slightly and then pour all the ingredients into a blender or food processor before blending.) Add a pinch of sea salt and black pepper to taste.

To make the croutons, heat a medium frying pan and butter one side of each slice of bread. Place one slice, butter-side down, in the frying pan and cover with the grated cheese.

Then place the second slice of bread, butter-side up, on top of the cheesy bread in the frying pan. Cook until golden brown on the underside, then flip the sandwich over to cook the other side. It needs about 2 minutes each side, until the outside of the sandwich is crisp and golden and the cheese has melted. Turn off the heat and transfer the sandwich to a chopping board. Using a sharp knife, cut the sandwich into small cubes to form croutons. Sprinkle a few croutons on top of each bowl of soup before serving.

COURGETTE AND LEEK FRITTERS
WITH FETA CITRUS DRESSING

MAKES 12 FRITTERS (2 per person), approx. 8cm in diameter
Prep time: 15 minutes
Cooking time: 10–12 minutes

INGREDIENTS
250g courgettes (about 2
   medium), trimmed
250g leeks (1 medium), trimmed
   and finely chopped
1 red onion, finely chopped
1 tablespoon finely chopped fresh
   dill, or 1 teaspoon dried dill
1 tablespoon finely chopped fresh
   parsley, or 1 teaspoon dried parsley
zest of 1 lemon
1 tablespoon nutritional yeast flakes
   or tamari (for gluten-free option)
   or soy sauce
100g buckwheat flour (for gluten-free
   option) or plain or spelt flour
3 eggs, beaten
sea salt and freshly ground black
   pepper, to taste
light olive oil or vegetable oil
   (approx. 4 tablespoons), for frying

For the dressing:
120g feta cheese, crumbled
3 tablespoons plain yoghurt
3 tablespoons freshly squeezed
   lemon juice (approx. 1½ lemons)

GF

Courgettes and leeks go so well together. These fritters have a good hit of lemon zest and fresh herbs so they are bursting with flavour. The feta citrus dressing is brilliantly tangy and great for dipping the fritters in or for drizzling on top.

METHOD
Preheat the oven to 160°C/gas mark 3. Grate the raw courgette and lay it evenly on a clean tea towel or sheet of kitchen paper, then roll up to soak away the excess juice. Set aside until ready to use.

To make the dressing, put the feta, yoghurt and lemon juice into a blender and whizz for about 10 seconds. Transfer to a serving bowl or jug and set to one side. If you do not have a blender, mash the ingredients together with a fork.

In a medium mixing bowl, combine the chopped leeks, red onion, dill, parsley, lemon zest and nutritional yeast flakes (or tamari or soy sauce). Stir in the flour and then the beaten egg. Finally stir in the grated courgette and season with a pinch of sea salt and freshly ground black pepper. Make sure all the ingredients are well mixed together.

Heat the oil over a medium-high heat in a large frying pan. There should be sufficient oil to just cover the base of the pan. When the oil is hot, take 1 dessertspoonful of the leek and courgette fritter mixture and spoon into the pan, then flatten the fritter with the back of the spoon so it is about 8cm wide. Continue with another 2 or 3 spoonfuls of mixture at a time, ensuring there is enough space in between to be able to turn your fritters.

Cook for about 2 minutes on each side, or until golden and cooked through. Drain on kitchen paper, then wrap in foil and keep warm in the oven while you make the rest of the fritters. Once you've cooked them all, serve them immediately, either with the dressing alongside in a small bowl for dipping, or drizzled over the top.

HERB AND CHEESE SOUFFLÉ

SERVES 4–6

Prep time: 30 minutes

Cooking time: 35–40 minutes

INGREDIENTS

40g butter, plus more for greasing
the dish

60g buckwheat flour (for gluten-free
option) or plain or spelt flour

400ml milk, at room temperature

1 teaspoon English or Dijon mustard

6 large eggs, separated

250g mature Cheddar or Gruyère

80g Parmesan

2 tablespoons of a combination of
three of the following fresh herbs,
finely chopped: sage, thyme,
oregano, marjoram, parsley

freshly ground black pepper, to taste

GF

Mum would often ask me to make her a cheese soufflé, so I grew up loving making them. The common perception is that soufflés are difficult to get right, but as long as you cook them properly they're pretty straightforward. For a dinner party, I make one large soufflé instead of individual ones. I prepare the cheese sauce ahead of time and then whisk the egg whites and stir them into the sauce just before I'm ready to put it in the oven. A main-course showstopper.

METHOD

Preheat the oven to 200°C/gas mark 6. Butter a 15cm soufflé dish or a similar-sized ovenproof dish.

You can prepare the cheese sauce in advance if you want to. To make the sauce, melt the butter in a medium pan over a medium heat. Stir in the flour, using a wooden spoon, until a firm paste is formed. Remove from the heat and add the milk a little at a time, stirring continuously with a hand whisk until there are no lumps. Place back on the heat and keep stirring until the sauce has thickened – about 4–5 minutes. Remove from the heat and allow to cool slightly before stirring in the mustard, egg yolks, cheeses, herbs and a little black pepper to taste. (You probably won't need salt as the cheese is quite salty already.) Transfer the sauce to a large mixing bowl.

To finish the soufflé, whisk the egg whites in a separate, clean bowl, using an electric whisk, until they form stiff peaks. Stir 2 heaped tablespoonfuls of the whisked egg whites into the cheese sauce to loosen and lighten it. Then gently fold in the rest of the whisked whites with a large metal spoon; a light touch is important so that you don't bash out the bubbles.

Gently pour this mixture into the prepared soufflé dish. Bake in the middle of the oven for 35–40 minutes (35 minutes if you like a slightly runny centre or 40 minutes for a firmer centre), until well risen and brown on top. This soufflé goes particularly well with the Wilted Spinach (p.182).

WILTED SPINACH

SERVES 6

Prep time: 1–2 minutes
Cooking time: 1 minute

INGREDIENTS

400g spinach, washed well
1 teaspoon extra-virgin olive oil
    or melted butter
squeeze of fresh lemon juice
small pinch sea salt
freshly ground black pepper, to taste

GF, V+, DF

A very simple side dish – and so nutritious. This is my favourite way to eat spinach and it forms a good counterbalance to the richness of the Herb and Cheese Soufflé (p.180). You can put this on to cook when the soufflé is almost ready.

METHOD

Put the spinach into a medium–large saucepan, cover and cook over a medium heat for 1–2 minutes, until all the leaves have just wilted. Drain well in a colander. While the spinach is draining, heat the olive oil or melted butter in the pan. Then add the wilted spinach, lemon juice and salt, and stir together. Season with black pepper and it's ready.

BAKED PLUMS WITH FRESH BASIL AND AMARETTI CRISP

SERVES 6
Prep time: 7 minutes
Cooking time: 20 minutes

INGREDIENTS
12 ripe plums (approx. 500g)
8 tablespoons maple syrup
8 fresh basil leaves, thinly sliced
80g amaretti biscuits, crushed

GF, V+, DF

This dessert is perfect for a last–minute dinner party because it's quick and easy to make. You can have everything prepared in advance and then just put the plums in the oven when you're ready to bake. Despite its simplicity, this is an impressive dessert which packs a real flavour punch and is so pretty and aromatic. (If you need this to be gluten-free, check that your amaretti biscuits are made with almonds and have no added flour.)

METHOD
Preheat the oven to 160C°C/gas mark 3. Cut the plums in half and remove the stones. Lay the plum halves, cut-side up, evenly on a medium baking tray. Drizzle with the maple syrup, then bake for 20 minutes until soft and juicy.

Remove from the oven and scatter the basil leaves over the baked plums, then sprinkle with the crushed amaretti biscuits. Transfer the plums to serving dish.

I think this pudding is delicious served with a spoon of crème fraîche, vanilla ice cream or soya cream.

BONFIRE

PARTY

BONFIRE PARTY

My family loves a bonfire. I have fond memories of my dad putting out bales of hay around the fire and we would sit together, warming ourselves by the flames, eating and telling stories. So when I thought about this menu, my head was full of crisp autumn evenings warmed by the glow of the bonfire flames. These are family-friendly, warming recipes to be enjoyed outside.

MENU

Incredibly Onion Soup with Garlic Toasts - GF, V+, DF

One-Pot Chilli with Baked Potatoes - GF, V+, DF

Apple Wedges with Caramel Dipping Sauce - GF, V+, DF

Ginger and Pine Nut Cookies - GF, DF

Luxury Hot Chocolate - GF, V+, DF

INCREDIBLY ONION SOUP
WITH GARLIC TOASTS

SERVES 6

Prep time: 15 minutes
Cooking time: 1 hour

INGREDIENTS

For the soup:

3 tablespoons light olive oil or
    vegetable oil

6 medium white onions (approx.
    600g), thinly sliced

1 medium leek (approx. 250g),
    trimmed and finely chopped

3 cloves garlic, finely chopped

1 teaspoon agave syrup or sugar

2 tablespoons buckwheat flour (for
    gluten-free option) or plain
    or spelt flour

500ml white wine

2 teaspoons dried thyme

1 teaspoon mustard, preferably Dijon

2 bay leaves

1 litre vegetable stock

For the garlic toasts:

1 baguette, or 6 slices gluten-free
    bread (allow 1 slice per serving)

3 tablespoons extra-virgin olive oil
    or melted butter

2 cloves garlic, crushed

1 tablespoon finely chopped
    fresh parsley

pinch sea salt

GF, V+, DF

Made with slow-cooked onions and topped with lucious garlic croutons, this soup is perfect for a cold autumn night.

METHOD

To make the soup, heat the oil in a large saucepan over a medium heat. Stir in the sliced onions, then turn down the heat to low, cover and cook gently for 10 minutes, stirring occasionally. Add the leek and the garlic and cook for a further 5 minutes.

Take the lid off, then add the syrup or sugar and allow it to cook very gently for a further 30 minutes, stirring often. You don't want the onions to go crisp, just golden brown and nicely caramelised.

Now stir in the flour, coating the onions, and heat through for 1 minute. Gradually stir in the white wine, thyme, mustard and bay leaves and bring to a gentle bubble. Then slowly pour in the vegetable stock and simmer gently for 30 minutes.

To make the garlic toasts, cut the bread into 2cm-thick slices. In a small bowl, mix the oil or butter with the crushed garlic, chopped parsley and a pinch of sea salt.

Grill the slices of bread on one side, then turn them over and spread the garlic mixture on to the other side. Put back under the grill, garlicky side up, for a few minutes until toasted.

Ladle or spoon the onion soup into bowls. Lay the garlic toasts on top of the hot onion soup and serve immediately.

ONE-POT CHILLI
WITH BAKED POTATOES

SERVES 6
Prep time: 15 minutes
Cooking time: 40–60 minutes

INGREDIENTS
6 baking potatoes

For the chilli sauce:
2 tablespoons light olive oil or
    vegetable oil
2 medium onions, finely chopped
2 cloves garlic, finely chopped
200g green beans, trimmed
    and chopped
1 red pepper, deseeded and
    finely chopped
400g tin kidney beans, drained
100g veggie mince or chopped up
    veggie burger (optional)
1–2 teaspoon chipotle chilli paste,
    or ½ teaspoon dried chilli flakes
2 x 400g tins chopped tomatoes
4 tablespoons water
1 tablespoon Worcestershire sauce
    (vegetarian, no anchovies)
1 tablespoon tamari (for gluten-free
    option) or soy sauce
1 tablespoon finely chopped fresh
    coriander or parsley, or 1 teaspoon
    dried herbs
sea salt and freshly ground black
    pepper, to taste
sour cream or crème fraîche (or
    dairy-free plain yoghurt), to serve

GF, V+, DF

Juicy, tangy, with a bit of chilli heat, and easy to make – this is a one-pot recipe so you won't have much washing up! I like to use chipotle chilli paste as it's made using smoked jalapeños and so adds a wonderful smoky flavour to the dish.

METHOD
Preheat the oven to 180°C/gas mark 4. Wash the potatoes and prick them with a fork. Wrap them in kitchen foil and bake in the oven – this should take about 1 hour, depending on the size of your potatoes.

Meanwhile, make the chilli sauce. Heat the oil in a medium to large saucepan, add the onions and fry gently for 5 minutes. Stir in the garlic, green beans and red pepper. Turn up the heat slightly, then stir in the drained kidney beans and the veggie mince (if using) and cook through for 1 minute.

Stir in the chipotle paste or chilli flakes, the chopped tomatoes, water, Worcestershire sauce and tamari or soy sauce. Bring to a gentle simmer, then cover and cook for 30 minutes, checking and stirring occasionally.

Taste, and add more seasoning as necessary. If you prefer a spicier sauce, add extra chipotle paste or chilli flakes. The sauce should be rich and thickened. Finally, stir in the herbs and add sea salt and black pepper to taste. Keep warm until the potatoes are ready.

To serve, spoon the chilli sauce evenly over the baked potatoes and top each one with a dollop of sour cream or crème fraîche.

APPLE WEDGES
WITH CARAMEL DIPPING SAUCE

SERVES 6

Prep time: 5 minutes

Cooking time: 10 minutes

INGREDIENTS

For the caramel dipping sauce:

200ml agave syrup

400ml single cream (or soya cream
for dairy-free option)

½ teaspoon ground cinnamon

For the apple wedges:

4 apples

24 wooden skewers

GF, V+, DF

For me, the flavours of apples and caramel conjure up images of autumn get-togethers. As children, we loved it when Mum and Dad got us bobbing for apples – brilliant bonfire party fun!

METHOD

To make the caramel dipping sauce, heat the agave syrup in a medium, heavy-bottomed saucepan. Bring it to a gentle bubble and then simmer for about 4 minutes. Be careful not to let it bubble too vigorously as you don't want it to burn. Letting it bubble gently will allow the sauce to thicken slightly when it cools.

Meanwhile, in a separate, small saucepan gently heat the cream and cinnamon together; it needs to be warm, as cold cream could curdle when mixed with the hot agave syrup.

When the agave syrup is ready, stir in the warm cinnamon cream and simmer for another minute. Take off the heat. At this point, you can use a hand whisk to combine the ingredients well. Pour the caramel sauce into a serving bowl.

Cut the apples into six wedges and cut away any core. Stick wooden skewers into the tops of the apple pieces. Now they're ready to dip into the sauce.

GINGER AND PINE NUT COOKIES

MAKES 24 COOKIES

Prep time: 20 minutes

Cooking time: 7–8 minutes per batch

INGREDIENTS

80g butter (or coconut oil for
   dairy-free option)

75g soft light brown sugar or
   coconut sugar

1 egg, beaten

60g molasses

175g buckwheat flour (for gluten-
   free option) or plain or spelt flour

¾ teaspoon baking powder

2 tablespoons ground ginger

1 teaspoon ground cinnamon

¼ teaspoon sea salt

70g pine nuts

icing sugar, for dusting the
   cookies (optional)

GF, DF

*These cookies deliver a gingery warming kick – ideal on a chilly night –
and the pine nuts give them extra creamy texture.*

METHOD:

Preheat the oven to 180°C/gas mark 4 and line two large baking
trays with greaseproof paper (or lightly grease them).

In a large mixing bowl or food processor, beat the butter and sugar
together until creamy. Mix in the beaten egg and molasses. Gradually
sift in the flour, baking powder, ground ginger and cinnamon and salt,
then add the pine nuts. Mix together until all the ingredients are well
combined and a stiff dough is formed.

Using 1 heaped teaspoonful of dough per cookie, roll the mixture
into balls and place on the baking trays, leaving a 3cm gap between
each cookie, then flatten them slightly with the back of the spoon.
Bake for 7–8 minutes, or until just cooked through and slightly crisp
at the edges but still soft on top.

Transfer the cookies to a wire rack and leave to cool. If you like, you
can dust with icing sugar before serving.

LUXURY HOT CHOCOLATE

SERVES 6

Prep time: 5 minutes

Cooking time: 5 minutes

INGREDIENTS

3 tablespoons good-quality
cocoa powder

4½ tablespoons light agave syrup

1½ tablespoons vanilla extract

1.5 litres milk (or almond, soya or
rice milk for dairy-free option)

GF, V+, DF

Chocolate makes me happy. I make a large batch of this chocolate milk and what isn't used on the night, I pour back into the milk container and keep chilled in the fridge so I can drink it throughout the week as cold chocolate milk.

METHOD

Mix the cocoa powder and agave syrup together in a bowl or mug, using a fork to make a smooth paste with no lumps. Stir in the vanilla extract. To thin out the chocolate paste, stir in 3 tablespoons of the milk and mix with the fork until well combined.

Now transfer the chocolate paste into a large saucepan. Using a wooden spoon, gradually stir in the remaining milk. Place over a medium heat until it is warmed through and just starting to come bubble. Pour into mugs and enjoy.

KEEPING OUT

THE COLD

KEEPING OUT THE COLD

I grew up in the countryside and I still try to spend as much time there as possible. This is the type of meal I love to cook after I come in from a brisk horse ride in the winter and I have several hungry, cold people to feed. For me, it is all about soulful comfort food that leaves you feeling satisfied and warm on those winter evenings. Here, I have drawn on the earthy tastes and flavours of autumn and winter's seasonal ingredients.

MENU

Chilli Pumpkin Soup - GF, V+, DF

Mushroom and Chestnut Pie - GF, V+, DF

Red and Green Cabbage Twist - GF, V+, DF

Buttery Carrots with Fresh Herbs - GF, V+, DF

Spiced Poached Pears - GF, V+, DF

Crème Anglaise - GF

CHILLI PUMPKIN SOUP

SERVES 6

Prep time: 15 minutes

Cooking time: 30 minutes

INGREDIENTS

2 tablespoons light olive oil or
   vegetable oil

2 medium white onions,
   roughly chopped

2 cloves garlic, chopped

1 carrot, chopped

1 stick celery, chopped

1kg pumpkin or butternut squash,
   peeled, deseeded and cubed

6 fresh sage leaves, or 1 teaspoon
   dried sage

1 medium red chilli, deseeded and
   chopped (or 2 if you like a little extra
   heat), or ½ teaspoon chilli flakes

1 medium sweet potato, peeled
   and chopped

400g tin butter beans, drained

1.4 litres vegetable stock

sea salt and freshly ground black
   pepper, to taste

pumpkin seeds, to garnish

drizzle of chilli oil or extra-virgin
   olive oil (optional)

spoonful of crème fraîche or soya
   cream (optional)

GF, V+, DF

My mum loved pumpkins; she and Dad grew them every year. So we would carve them for Hallowe'en, but we also cooked many pumpkin recipes throughout the season. I love the combination of pumpkin with a hint of chilli heat. Use more or less chilli, depending on how hot you like it.

METHOD

Heat the oil in a large, heavy-bottomed saucepan over a medium heat, then add the onions, garlic, carrot and celery and sauté for a couple of minutes. Next, add the chopped pumpkin, sage, chilli, sweet potato and butter beans and continue to cook for a further 2 minutes.

Add the vegetable stock, stir and bring to the boil, then turn down the heat to a gentle simmer. Cover with a lid and cook for 25 minutes, or until all the vegetables and beans have softened and cooked through.

Allow to cool slightly before whizzing with a stick blender in the pan. (If blending in a food processor, let the soup cool slightly, then ladle in small amounts and blend a bit at a time.)

Toast the pumpkin seeds in a small, dry frying pan, over a medium heat, until they go crisp – about 3 minutes. Don't let them burn. Take off the heat.

To serve, sprinkle a few toasted pumpkin seeds on top of each bowl of soup and drizzle with a little oil and thinly sliced red chilli, if desired, or a little crème fraîche.

MUSHROOM AND CHESTNUT PIE

SERVES 6

Prep time: 20 minutes

Cooking time: 1 hour

INGREDIENTS

For the filling:

2 tablespoons light olive oil or
   vegetable oil

2 medium leeks (approx. 300g),
   finely chopped

1 medium red onion, finely chopped

300g chestnut mushrooms or similar,
   thinly sliced

250g cooked and peeled
   chestnuts, quartered

2 tablespoons tamari or soy sauce

1 tablespoon vegetarian
   Worcestershire sauce

1 tablespoon finely chopped fresh
   sage, or 1 teaspoon dried sage

1 tablespoon finely chopped fresh
   thyme, or 1 teaspoon dried thyme

2 tablespoons finely chopped fresh
   rosemary, or 1 tablespoon
   dried rosemary

1 tablespoon cornflour

1½ tablespoons vegetable
   stock powder

400ml cold water

1½ teaspoons mustard, preferably
   English or Dijon

freshly ground black pepper, to taste

For the pastry:

320g ready-rolled puff pastry
   (you can find gluten-free)

flour, for rolling

a little milk or beaten egg (or almond
   milk), for brushing on top

GF, V+, DF

This is a wonderful traditional pie made using one large piece of puff pastry folded around a mushroom and chestnut gravy filling – easy to make and a great centrepiece to this meal. You can assemble the pie an hour ahead, then brush with milk or beaten egg just before baking.

METHOD

Preheat the oven to 200°C/gas mark 6. You will need a 23cm round pie dish for this recipe.

To make the filling, gently heat the oil in a large, deep-sided frying pan or medium saucepan. Add the leeks, onion, mushrooms, chestnuts, tamari or soy sauce and Worcestershire sauce. Sauté for about 12 minutes over a medium-high heat, stirring often. Add the herbs and cook for a further 2–3 minutes, then turn the heat down slightly.

Meanwhile, make the vegetable stock by adding the cornflour and vegetable stock powder to a mixing jug, then stirring in the cold water and mixing well. (Don't use hot water or your stock will go lumpy.)

Gradually pour the vegetable stock into the leek and mushroom mixture, stirring gently with a wooden spoon until the mixture reaches a gentle simmer. Add the mustard and cook, stirring often, for a further 8 minutes or so. It should thicken into a glossy sauce. Season with black pepper to taste and set aside to come to room temperature, about 15 minutes.

Unroll the puff pastry sheet on a clean, lightly floured surface. Gently roll out the pastry a little more until it is about 2–3mm thick – there needs to be a larger surface area of dough to hang over the edges of the pastry tin – you will need this for when you come to fold it over the filling to close the top of the pie. Loosely line the inside of your pie dish with the pastry, leaving the extra pastry hanging over the edges (a quiche tin with a detachable base works well if you want to transfer the pie to a serving dish when cooked).

When the mushroom and chestnut filling has cooled, spoon it onto the pastry base and gently spread it evenly around. Now fold the edges of the excess pastry into the centre, over the filling, to close the pie. Lightly pinch the edges together so it stays closed. Brush the top of the pie with milk or beaten egg and bake for 35 minutes (allow an extra 5–10 minutes if baking from fridge-cold), until the top of the pie is golden brown.

RED AND GREEN CABBAGE TWIST

SERVES 6

Prep time: 10 minutes
Cooking time: 10 minutes

INGREDIENTS

1 tablespoon light olive oil or
   vegetable oil

½ red onion, halved and thinly sliced

2 garlic cloves, finely chopped

1–2 teaspoons caraway seeds, to taste

220g green cabbage (approx. ½
   cabbage), such as Savoy, shredded

220g red cabbage (approx. ⅓
   cabbage), shredded

zest of 1 lemon

pinch sea salt and freshly ground
   black pepper, to taste

GF, V+, DF

The mixture of green and red cabbage makes for a fabulously colourful side dish that complements the earthy colours of the mushroom and chestnut pie so well. Cabbage doesn't have a good culinary reputation, but cooked properly, it's delicious – and also one of the healthiest vegetables you can eat.

METHOD

Heat the oil in a large frying pan over a medium heat. Add the onion and garlic and turn the heat down to low – this will prevent the garlic and onions from burning – then cook for 3–4 minutes until softened.

Add the caraway seeds and green and red cabbage and turn the heat back up to medium so you can hear a nice sizzle. Cook, mixing often, for 5–7 minutes until the cabbage is lightly cooked but still a little crunchy. Season with a pinch of sea salt and black pepper to taste. Turn off the heat. Mix in the lemon zest, and it's ready to serve.

BUTTERY CARROTS
WITH FRESH HERBS

SERVES 6

Prep time: 7 minutes
Cooking time: 11 minutes

INGREDIENTS

500g carrots, cut into 4cm batons
80g butter or olive oil
pinch sea salt
100ml water (or enough to nearly
  cover the carrots in the pan)
squeeze of lemon juice
1 tablespoon finely chopped fresh
  herbs, such as tarragon, parsley,
  thyme or marjoram

GF, V+, DF

A nutritious side dish that adds wonderful colour to the meal. Adding butter to the cooking water gives the carrots a lovely glossy glaze which makes them look and taste special.

METHOD

Lay the carrot batons in a layer in a large frying pan or saucepan, one that has a lid. Add the butter (or oil), a pinch of salt and the water. Bring to the boil, cover and cook for about 7 minutes, or until the carrots are tender. Make sure the pan does not completely dry out; you may need to add a little more water from time to time.

When the carrots are just cooked, remove the lid and reduce the cooking liquid until thick enough to glaze the carrots – this should take around 4 minutes. Turn off the heat and drain away any excess liquid. Squeeze a little lemon juice over the carrots, followed by a scattering of fresh herbs. Mix together well, and serve.

SPICED POACHED PEARS

SERVES 6
Prep time: 15 minutes,
Cooking time: 45 minutes
Cooling time: 2 hours

INGREDIENTS
1 bottle (750ml) red wine
 (preferably Burgundy)
400ml water
1 stick cinnamon
1 vanilla pod, split lengthways with
 seeds scraped out, or 1 tablespoon
 vanilla extract
pared zest of 1 unwaxed lemon
 (use a potato peeler)
pared zest of 1 unwaxed orange
 (use a potato peeler)
4 whole cloves
3 tablespoons agave syrup
6 firm ripe pears

To serve (optional):
Crème Anglaise (p.221)

GF, V+, DF

The seasonal spice in this simple dessert delivers a spectacular taste sensation. There are many varieties of pear, and for this recipe you want to choose one that will remain firm when poached. The cooking time will vary, depending on the firmness of your pears, so after about 10 minutes of poaching it's best to test them every few minutes; if you overcook them they will fall apart, and undercooked they will be too crisp. Test by sticking in a skewer to make sure the pear is just tender all the way through. This is great served with the Crème Anglaise (p.221) - or natural coconut milk yoghurt for a dairy-free option.

METHOD
In a large saucepan (big enough to hold all of the pears), place all of the ingredients (except for the pears). Bring to the boil, and then reduce the heat and gently simmer for 10 minutes.

Meanwhile, slice the bottom off the pears slightly, to allow them to sit upright on a flat surface without tipping over. Then, using a melon baller, small knife or teaspoon, gently scoop the core out from the bottom of the pear. Finally, peel the pears, leaving the stems on.

Gently place the pears upright in the simmering liquid and poach for 10-15 minutes, depending on the firmness of the pears (test them after 10 minutes). Turn off the heat and leave them to cool in the liquid for 2 hours. This will soften the pears further and allow them to soak up all the flavours of the liquid.

After the pears have finished cooling to room temperature and soaking in the liquid, gently remove them and arrange on serving plates or in bowls. Serve with the Crème Anglaise, if desired.

Note: You can remove and discard all the flavourings (cinnamon stick, and peel and cloves) from the poaching liquid and keep the liquid (which can be chilled or frozen) for poaching more pears at a later date.

CRÈME ANGLAISE

SERVES 6

Prep time: 12 minutes
Cooking time: 10 minutes

INGREDIENTS

400g single or double cream
1 vanilla pod, split lengthways,
   or 1 tablespoon vanilla extract
5 large egg yolks
70g sugar

GF

This luxuriously creamy pouring vanilla sauce, which I cannot resist, is the perfect match for the Spiced Poached Pears (p.218). I guess you could just call it custard, but I think the French name sounds a bit more exotic!

METHOD

In a medium saucepan, gently heat the cream and vanilla pod (or extract) until bubbles just begin to form around the edges of the pan, then turn off the heat and allow the infused cream to cool slightly. Remove the vanilla pod if using (being careful not to burn your fingers) and scrape out the seeds with either a butter knife or a metal teaspoon. Put these vanilla seeds back into the cream and discard the pod.

Beat the egg yolks and sugar together in a medium mixing bowl until light and frothy. Using a hand whisk, mix a couple of tablespoons of the cooled cream and vanilla mixture into the egg yolks, before gradually whisking in the rest. Pour the mixture back into the saucepan over a low to medium heat. Stir gently with a wooden spoon until the mixture thickens enough to coat the back of the spoon. To serve, strain through a sieve into a jug, to give a smoother consistency.

NB: If the mixture starts to curdle, add a little extra cream and beat gently with a hand whisk until the texture has evened out.

This is also amazing poured over fruit pies, or steamed puddings.

FESTIVE
FEAST

FESTIVE FEAST

Where my dad grew up, the Sunday roast was a weekly tradition and a big family occasion. And when we were growing up as vegetarians, my mum and dad were keen to continue the custom of having the family gather round the table for a Sunday feast, vegetarian-style, so we never felt we were missing out. I've borne this in mind when planning this festive menu, which is special enough for the Big Day: a mouthwatering veggie roast with all the trimmings – stuffing, roast vegetables, mashed potatoes, a luscious red wine gravy, a side of vegetables and an indulgent chocolate dessert.

MENU

Festive Roast - GF, DF

Celebration Stuffing - GF, V+, DF

Roasted Root Vegetables with Rosemary - GF, V+, DF

Baked Broccoli and Cauliflower Florets - GF, V+, DF

Hot Brussels Sprout Coleslaw - GF, V+, DF

Mashed Potatoes Topped with Caramelised Leeks - GF

Red Wine Gravy - GF, V+, DF

Chocolate and Cherry Roulade

FESTIVE ROAST

SERVES 6–8
Prep time: 30 minutes
Cooking time: 45 minutes

INGREDIENTS

50g raw cashew nuts, chopped small

50 raw almonds, chopped small

50g sunflower seeds, roughly chopped

2 tablespoons tamari (for gluten-free option) or soy sauce

2 tablespoons light olive oil or vegetable oil, plus more for greasing the tin

2 medium onions, finely chopped

1 stick celery, finely chopped

2 cloves garlic, finely chopped

200ml tinned chopped tomatoes

1 carrot, grated

160g cooked puy lentils (or tinned aduki beans, drained)

1 tablespoon chopped fresh thyme, or 1 teaspoon dried thyme

1 tablespoon chopped fresh rosemary, or 1 teaspoon dried rosemary

1 tablespoon chopped fresh sage, or 1 teaspoon dried sage

200g cooked white quinoa

3 tablespoons nutritional yeast flakes, or 1 tablespoon Marmite

2 tablespoon buckwheat flour (for gluten-free option) or plain or spelt flour

50g dried cranberries (optional)

2 large eggs, beaten

freshly ground black pepper, to taste

GF, DF

I've worked on this recipe over the years and feel it makes a tasty centrepiece for a roast dinner. You can prepare the veggie roast mix the day before and keep it chilled in the fridge. It goes well with roast vegetables and all the traditional trimmings, with a generous pouring of gravy over the top. I suggest you have a dollop of horseradish sauce on the side, too. This recipe serves six to eight, so double the quantities and cook in two loaf tins if you are making it for a larger gathering. I like to have some left over so I can use it in a sandwich the next day with some Thousand Island dressing (p.79) and crisp lettuce leaves.

METHOD

Preheat the oven to 180°C/gas mark 4. Grease and line a 23 x 13cm loaf tin with greaseproof paper, then brush a little oil on the paper too.

In a dry, heavy-bottomed frying pan over a medium heat, toast the chopped cashews, almonds and sunflower seeds for 2–3 minutes until lightly browned. Add the tamari or soy sauce and toss to coat the nuts. Remove from the heat and tip the toasted nuts and seeds into a large mixing bowl. Set aside and leave to cool.

In the same frying pan, heat the oil and gently fry the onions and celery for 10 minutes until golden and cooked through. Add the garlic, chopped tomatoes, grated carrot and cooked lentils (or aduki beans), mix well and sauté for a couple of minutes, then tip into the bowl containing the toasted nuts and mix together. Add the herbs and the remaining ingredients to the bowl and mix until well combined. Season with black pepper to taste.

When you are ready to cook, transfer your mixture to the prepared loaf tin and bake for 30 minutes. Remove from the oven and turn out onto a baking tray. Peel off the greaseproof paper, then put the roast back into the oven for a further 15 minutes until golden and cooked through. Let it rest for 5 minutes before slicing – this will allow it to firm up slightly and make it easier to slice. Place on a serving dish and cut into slices with a sharp carving or bread knife.

CELEBRATION STUFFING

SERVES 6–8
Prep time: 20 minutes
Cooking time: 45 minutes

INGREDIENTS
3 slices sandwich bread (approx.
    120g), cut into 2.5cm cubes
100g butter, or 4 tablespoons light
    olive oil or vegetable oil, plus more
    for greasing the trays/dish
2 onions, finely chopped
1 leek, trimmed and finely chopped
2 sticks celery, finely chopped
1 pear, cored and chopped
    into 1cm pieces
1 tablespoon finely chopped
    fresh rosemary
2 tablespoons finely chopped
    fresh sage
1 tablespoon finely chopped
    fresh parsley
100g pine nuts
1 large egg, beaten (optional)
250ml vegetable stock
freshly ground black pepper, to taste
sea salt, to taste (optional; you may
    not need extra salt if your stock is
    already salty)

GF, V+, DF

My mum taught me how to make stuffing. The basics are bread, celery, onions and herbs. You can make it into balls to bake, or as one whole piece in a baking dish. Gluten-free bread will work here too, as long as it is a light loaf, not too heavy, and if you want a vegan option you can leave out the beaten egg. No festive roast is complete without stuffing, and this recipe fits the bill perfectly. You can prepare it in advance and simply reheat it in the oven when needed.

METHOD
Preheat the oven to 180°C/gas mark 4. If making balls of stuffing, lightly grease two baking trays; if baking in one piece, grease a 24 x 24cm baking dish.

Spread the cubes of bread on a baking tray and bake for 10 minutes until crisp. Meanwhile, in a large, heavy-bottomed pan, melt the butter or heat the oil over a medium to low heat. Add the onions, leek, celery and pear and sauté for about 15 minutes until softened and golden.

Mix in the toasted bread cubes, the herbs and pine nuts, and season with black pepper and sea salt to taste. Stir in the vegetable stock and the beaten egg, if using, and leave for 10 minutes to thoroughly soak in.

If making stuffing balls, scoop up 1 dessertspoonful of stuffing at a time, then mould it into a ball and place on your prepared baking tray. Or, if baking in one piece, simply press the stuffing mix gently into your prepared baking dish.

Bake the stuffing for 25-30 minutes (25 minutes for balls and 30 minutes if baking in one piece) until crisp and golden on the outside, but still soft on the inside.

ROASTED ROOT VEGETABLES
WITH ROSEMARY

SERVES 6
Prep time: 10 minutes
Cooking time: 65 minutes

INGREDIENTS

500g carrots (approx. 6
    medium), halved

500g parsnips (approx. 6 medium),
    trimmed and halved

12 new potatoes or small potatoes,
    halved (or 4 small turnips, trimmed
    and halved)

3 medium sweet potatoes, quartered

2 red onions, quartered

1 head garlic, halved

4 rosemary sprigs

3 tablespoons light olive oil
    or vegetable oil

2 pinches sea salt and freshly ground
    black pepper, to taste

GF, V+, DF

A fantastic combination of root vegetables is an essential part of any festive meal. I heap them all together on a serving dish and let my guests serve themselves. The vegetables can be prepared and parboiled then set aside until you're ready to pop them into the oven to roast.

METHOD

Preheat the oven to 180°C/gas mark 4. Put the carrots, parsnips, small potatoes (or turnips) and sweet potatoes into a large pan of cold salted water. Bring to the boil then turn the heat down to medium. Cook for 5 minutes and then drain in a colander. If you are preparing ahead of time, you can now keep in the refrigerator until you are ready to roast the vegetables.

Lay the parboiled vegetables, along with the onions, garlic and rosemary, on a large baking tray or divide between two trays. The vegetables will crisp up better if the tray isn't overcrowded. Drizzle with the oil, add a sprinkle of sea salt and toss together so that the vegetables are lightly coated in the oil.

About 15 minutes before you start to cook your festive roast, pop the vegetables in the oven and roast for 1 hour, making sure to toss after 30 minutes and, if using two trays, switching their position in the oven. Serve the roasted vegetables immediately, seasoned with a little black pepper if desired.

233

BAKED BROCCOLI AND CAULIFLOWER FLORETS

SERVES 6
Prep time: 5 minutes
Cooking time: 40 minutes

INGREDIENTS

1 large head broccoli (approx. 350g)
½ medium to large head cauliflower
1 tablespoon olive oil
½ teaspoon sea salt
squeeze of lemon, to serve

GF, V+, DF

A very easy side dish – I like to roast the broccoli and cauliflower, as it means I can just chuck it in the oven for 40 minutes before we eat. No fuss but full of flavour and full of goodness too. If you make a little too much, any leftovers can be turned into a great salad the next day. Simply sprinkle with toasted flaked almonds or pumpkin seeds, then drizzle with a little olive oil, a squeeze of lemon juice and a pinch of sea salt.

METHOD

Preheat the oven to 180°C/gas mark 4 and get out a medium to large baking dish.

Break the broccoli and cauliflower into florets, rinse them with cold water and leave them slightly damp as this will help the vegetables to steam and cook once in the oven. Lay them in your baking dish, drizzle with the olive oil and sprinkle with sea salt. Toss to ensure all the florets are lightly coated.

Cover the baking dish with foil and bake the vegetables in the oven for 20 minutes. Remove the foil, stir and cook for a further 20 minutes to allow them to brown slightly.

I love these with a squeeze of lemon juice.

HOT BRUSSELS SPROUT COLESLAW

SERVES 4–6
Prep time: 10 minutes
Cooking time: 3 minutes

INGREDIENTS

1 tablespoon wholegrain mustard
2 tablespoons white wine vinegar
1 tablespoon runny honey (or
  agave syrup)
2 tablespoons extra-virgin olive oil
400g Brussels sprouts, trimmed and
  thinly sliced
1 tablespoon chopped fresh parsley
sea salt and freshly ground black
  pepper, to taste

GF, V+, DF

This is the one and only way I like to eat Brussels sprouts. I've never been fond of them, but with this recipe I polish them off, no problem. They are stir-fried to retain their crispness and then tossed in a mustard, honey and white wine vinegar dressing. Now, I actually have to admit I like them! You can trim and slice the Brussels sprouts and make the dressing ahead of time, then set aside until you're ready to stir-fry.

METHOD

In a large bowl, whisk together the mustard, white wine vinegar and honey.

Heat a large frying pan until hot, add the oil and toss in the Brussels sprouts. Cook for 2 minutes, shaking the pan, until the sprouts are just starting to colour. Add the dressing and cook for a further minute. Turn off the heat then toss in the parsley and season with salt and pepper. Transfer to a warmed dish and serve immediately.

MASHED POTATOES
TOPPED WITH CARAMELISED LEEKS

SERVES 6

Prep time: 10 minutes

Cooking time: 25 minutes

INGREDIENTS

6 medium potatoes

1 tablespoon light olive oil or
    vegetable oil

1 large leek, trimmed and thinly sliced

200ml milk

100g butter

1 tablespoon horseradish
    sauce (optional)

sea salt and freshly ground black
    pepper, to taste

GF

Luxurious mashed potatoes are a classic. They're finished off here with gorgeous, slow-cooked leeks. I sometimes like to stir in a dollop of horseradish sauce for a little extra kick. Any leftovers can been rolled into patty shapes and shallow-fried until golden brown, then served with a poached egg on top.

METHOD

Peel and chop the potatoes into 3cm cubes. Place in a large saucepan of cold water, bring to the boil and then turn down to a gentle simmer for 20 minutes or until cooked through. Drain in a colander.

Meanwhile, to prepare the leeks, heat the oil in a heavy-bottomed frying pan, then add the sliced leek and a pinch of sea salt. Cook over a low-medium heat for 10-12 minutes, or until caramelised and lightly golden. Turn off the heat.

Once the potatoes are cooked and drained, tip them back into the large saucepan. Pour the milk over them and add the butter, then place over a low heat. Mash these ingredients together with a potato masher until they are smooth and there are no lumps. Then whisk lightly through with a fork to ensure they are light and fluffy. Stir in the horseradish sauce now, if using. Season with a pinch of sea salt and plenty of black pepper to taste, then transfer to a warmed serving dish and top with the caramelised leeks.

RED WINE GRAVY

SERVES 6
Prep time: 10 minutes
Cooking time: 15 minutes

INGREDIENTS
2 tablespoons light olive oil or
   vegetable oil
1 medium onion, thinly sliced
150g mushrooms, thinly sliced
1½ tablespoons cornflour
800ml vegetable stock
   (room temperature)
1 tablespoon chopped fresh thyme,
   or 1 teaspoon dried thyme
200ml red wine
40g frozen peas (optional)
salt and freshly ground black pepper,
   to taste

GF, V+, DF

I absolutely love gravy and it's so easy to make. I used to buy gravy granules but this simple recipe means you never have to again. You can prepare the gravy in advance and reheat it when you're ready to eat. I often make extra so I can freeze it and then defrost it as and when I need it. It's delicious poured over the festive roast, mashed potatoes and roast vegetables and, if you have some left over, it's also fantastic over mashed potatoes with veggie sausages the next day. The list goes on…

METHOD
Heat the oil in a medium saucepan and then sauté the onion and mushrooms for 5 minutes until softened. Mix the cornflour into the onion and mushroom mix and then gradually pour in the vegetable stock, stirring all the time with a wooden spoon to avoid lumps.

Add the thyme and red wine and cook for 7–10 minutes on a gentle simmer, stirring often, until the gravy has thickened. You want it to be thick enough to coat the back of the spoon.

Add the frozen peas, if using, then cook for a further minute. Season with salt and pepper to taste, before serving.

CHOCOLATE AND CHERRY ROULADE

SERVES 6

Prep time: 20 minutes

Cooling time: 20–30 minutes

Cooking time: 12 minutes

INGREDIENTS

For the base:

vegetable oil, for greasing the tin

6 large eggs, separated

175g caster sugar

50g cocoa powder, sifted, plus more
   for dusting the tin

2 tablespoons cherry brandy, for
   drizzling over the base (optional)

For the filling:

300ml double cream

2 teaspoons vanilla extract

140g good-quality cherry jam
   (Dalfour is good as it's made with
   natural fruit sugars)

440g tinned stoned black cherries,
   drained (or cherries soaked in Kirsch
   if you want a more boozy dessert)

For the topping:

1 teaspoon icing sugar, for dusting

80g dark chocolate (minimum 70%
   cocoa solids) or milk chocolate

6 tablespoons milk or single cream

This dessert looks simply stunning with all of its chocolate creaminess, and the cherries add extra juiciness. If you don't have, or don't want to use cherries, you can make this your own way, substituting something like fresh berries of your choice, or chopped pecan nuts, or even milk chocolate chips. Once again, it's about a creating a festive centrepiece, a real showoff dessert. If you're making this just for adults, then it's nice to use cherries in Kirsch for that extra kick. If I'm making this for children, I leave out the brandy.

METHOD

Preheat the oven to 180°C/gas mark 4. Lightly grease a 32 x 24cm swiss roll tin, line it, then brush the paper with oil and dust with cocoa powder.

First make the base. Add the sugar to the egg yolks in a medium bowl, and beat together until pale and creamy. Mix in the cocoa powder.

In a second bowl, whisk the egg whites together with a clean electric whisk until they form stiff peaks. Add 1 tablespoon of the whipped egg whites to the cocoa mixture, to loosen the consistency, then gently fold in the rest of the whites with a metal spoon until evenly mixed, being careful not to knock out the bubbles .Pour into the prepared tin, level the surface and bake for 12 minutes, or until the top is springy to the touch - do not overcook or the base will be too dry.

If using cherry brandy, sprinkle it evenly over the sponge at this point. Soak a clean tea towel in cold water and wring out until almost dry, then place over the cooked sponge in the baking tray (this helps to keep the sponge soft) and leave the sponge to cool for 20-30 minutes. Meanwhile, make the filling. Whip the cream until it is just firm and holds its shape, then mix in the vanilla extract.

Turn out the sponge onto the damp tea towel on a clean work surface. Now gently peel away the greaseproof paper. Spread the cherry jam over the base of the sponge, then spoon the whipped cream evenly over the jam, spreading it with a knife (leaving a 2cm gap around the edge). Dot with the cherries (or other berries of your choice, or chopped nuts or milk chocolate chips).

Now roll up your sponge. Lift the tea towel and tuck under the front edges and start to roll carefully, using the tea towel to help you lift and roll the chocolate base in on itself. Using two large spatulas, carefully transfer the roulade onto a serving plate. Use a sieve to dust the top with icing sugar. Melt the dark chocolate and the milk (or cream) together in a heatproof bowl set over a pan of simmering water, until it becomes a well-blended, smooth chocolate sauce.

Drizzle the sauce over the roulade and leave somewhere cool until ready to serve.

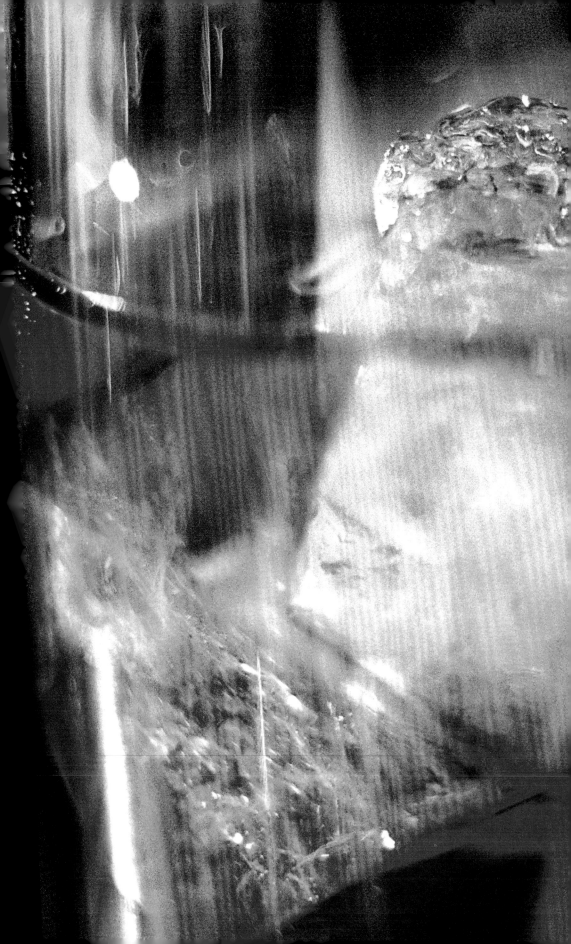

CONVERSION TABLES

WEIGHT

Ounces (oz)	Grams (g)
½	15
1	25
1½	45
2	55
2½	70
3	85
4	115
5	140
6	170
7	200
8	225
12	340
1lb	455
1lb 8oz	680
2lb	910

LIQUIDS

Fl.oz (pints)	Millilitres (litres)
2	60
3	90
4	120
5 (¼ pint)	140
6	180
7	205
8	230
10 (½ pint)	290
12	340
14	400
15	430
20 (1 pint)	570
2 pints	1.1l
1 tablespoon	(½ fl.oz/15ml)
2 tablespoons	(1 fl.oz/30ml)
3 tablespoons	(1½ fl.oz/45ml)
4 tablespoons	(2 fl.oz/60ml)
6 tablespoons	(3 fl.oz/85ml)
8 tablespoons	(4 fl.oz/115ml)

OVEN TEMPERATURES

°F	°C	Gas Mark
275	140	1
300	150	2
325	160/170	3
350	180	4
375	190	5
400	200	6
425	220	7

ACKNOWLEDGEMENTS

Simon, my beautiful boys Arthur, Elliot, Sam and Sid, the lovely Tabby, my little sister Stella, my big sister Heather, my little brother James and the Abouds.

And Alan Aboud, Polly Arber, Kim Bull, George Clark, Caroline Cortizo, Amanda Cross, Lee Eastman, Nathan Fuller, Tracy Gilbert, Poppy Hampson, Samantha Humble-Smith, Georgia Osner, Ciara Parkes, Glenn Wassall, Jo Woolhead, Kasia Zdanowska.

INDEX